MARTHA STEWART'S
Crafts for all
Occasions

MARTHA STEWART'S
Crafts for all
Occasions

With 225 projects for New Year's through
Christmas, and every celebration in between

D&C
David and Charles

A DAVID & CHARLES BOOK
David & Charles is an imprint of F&W Media International, LTD
Brunel House, Forde Close, Newton Abbot, TQ12 4PU, UK

Originally published in the United States by Potter Craft,
an imprint of the Crown Publishing Group,
a division of Random House, Inc., New York
www.crownpublishing.com
www.pottercraft.com

First published in the UK in 2011 by F&W Media International, LTD
F&W Media International, LTD is a subsidiary of F+W Media, Inc.
4700 East Galbraith Road, Cincinnati, OH 45236

Portions of this work were originally published
in *Martha Stewart Living* magazine.

A catalogue record for this book is available from the British Library.

ISBN-13: 978-1-4463-0176-0 hardback
ISBN-10: 1-4463-0176-1 hardback

Printed in the United States of America

Front cover photographs by Ditte Isager (inset) and Johnny Miller
Spine photographs by Ditte Isager (top) and Sang An (bottom)
Back cover photographs (clockwise from left) by Sang An, Raymond Hom, Sivan Lewin, Gentl & Hyers, Sang An, Johnny
Miller, Maria Robledo, Antoine Bootz, and Johnny Miller

A list of photography credits appears on page 367.

10 9 8 7 6 5 4 3 2 1

F+W Media Inc. publishes high quality books on a wide range
of subjects. For more great book ideas visit: www.rucraft.co.uk

To the celebration of holidays and to the crafts
enthusiasts who create and do all the things that
make the occasions so special and meaningful

10

112

218

28

138

254

66

156

272

178

CONTENTS

INTRODUCTION

There is something magical, endearing, charming, and so heartfelt about the handmade, the homemade. Since the very first issue of *Martha Stewart Living,* it has been a priority to develop, design, and create—with our very own hands—evocative, personal, and beautiful objects that illustrate our love of, and dedication to, the celebration of the holidays.

Over the years, our crafts editors have been involved in the planning and making of thousands of amazing things that speak to our celebration of Christmas, Hanukkah, New Year's, and many other significant days throughout the calendar year. We have made untold numbers of Valentines, not only those meant for that "special someone" but also for children and colleagues and caregivers, and even for cats! We have dyed and decorated so many different eggs for Easter that we long ago lost count, but we haven't stopped thinking of beautiful new ways to embellish them. We have draped miles of stars-and-stripes-covered bunting and flags and swags over fences and railing and porches, all to proudly display our patriotism every Independence Day. We have made turkeys—lots of them—in honor of our national celebration of thanks: pom-pom turkeys, gilded resin turkeys, and so many more. And you can't imagine how many different things we've glittered for the holidays!

In this book, you will find the best of that assortment with fine illustrations, glorious photographs, and clear instructions showing you, step by step, how to fashion each wonderful object. This is a special book for people whose fingers itch to make and do, and I think that by completing these projects, our appreciation of the holidays and their real meaning, both religious and secular, is enhanced and invigorated. Enjoy!

Martha Stewart

Around the world, across the globe, the arrival of a new year marks the passage of time. The countdown to midnight is a celebration of the ephemeral, allowing us at once to look back with nostalgia and to look ahead—happily, hopefully, expectantly. New Year's festivities often focus on grand gestures: dressing up in black-tie, watching the ball drop, opening a bottle of bubbly. Yet crafting for New Year's is less about large-scale moments than it is about the personal touches that can set your fête apart from the endless stream of others. In other words, it's all in the details. With just a few inexpensive, easily accessible items, you can fashion **D.I.Y. PARTY SUPPLIES** like confetti bags, swizzle sticks, and noisemakers. **SETTING THE SCENE** with bright and cheerful paper garlands, streamers, and other fun, festive accoutrements is designed to help capture the spirit of this enchanted evening, however briefly. The magic of New Year's—like the bubbles that rise from a Champagne glass, and like time itself—is fleeting. Grab it while you can.

PREVIOUS Paper Party Hats, see page 14 for how-to

D.I.Y. PARTY SUPPLIES

EMBELLISHED PARTY ACCESSORIES Drinks? Check. Hors d'oeuvres? Check. You're well stocked, but New Year's Eve is not complete without horns, noisemakers, and a little confetti. These handcrafted supplies help transform a pleasant evening into a floor-stomping celebration when the clock strikes twelve. For instructions on how to create the party favors, see page 15.

Happy New Year!

paper party hats

Party hats aren't just for kids' birthdays. Crafted from patterned and metallic papers, our pointy, fringed chapeaus are plenty stylish—and just silly enough to encourage guests of all ages to cut loose. Chin straps will hold the hats in place, even if things take a raucous turn.

WHAT YOU WILL NEED Decorative paper (one sheet of metallic and one sheet of patterned for each hat), cutting mat, masking tape, adjustable circle cutter, scissors, white craft glue, small paintbrush, ⅛-inch hole punch, ¼-inch-wide metallic ribbon, tissue paper, fringe scissors, drinking straw

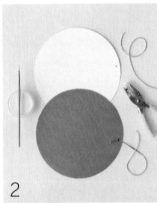

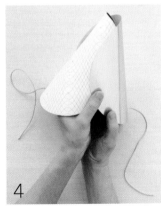

1 Use an adjustable circle cutter to cut one 8¼-inch circle from metallic paper and another from patterned paper. (Tape paper to cutting mat with masking tape to hold it in place while you cut.)

2 Glue one circle to the other so that they overlap by one-third. Let dry. Punch a hole in each circle ¼ inch from the edge, as shown. Thread each hole with a 12-inch length of ribbon, leaving a small overhang. Knot overhang, and glue to paper to secure; let dry.

3 For the tassel, cut out a 9-by-3-inch strip of tissue paper. Using fringe scissors (or regular scissors), cut slits along one long side of the rectangle, stopping an inch short of the opposite long side. Place drinking straw along a short side of the strip. Roll tissue paper around the straw once. Apply a line of glue along the long edge of the strip. Roll strip tightly around the straw, then glue to secure end. Remove straw.

4 Bring the outside edges of the hat together, forming a cone shape (hole at top should be about ¼ inch). Glue in place (hold down with your thumbs if needed). Secure the tassel to the top of the hat with glue; let dry.

embellished party accessories

Even the most basic crafting materials can transform everyday party supplies into something more memorable. The materials aren't hard to come by; you'll find them at party-supply stores, discount retailers, and office-supply centers. These accessories are small, but they're sure to make a big impression on your guests.

WHAT YOU WILL NEED Store-bought horns and noisemakers, tissue paper, scissors, fringe scissors, washi tape (available online), star-shaped paper punch, metallic card stock, glue dots, blue card stock, cellophane bags, confetti, ⅛-inch hole punch, blue raffia (or thin ribbon or twine), metal-rimmed paper tag

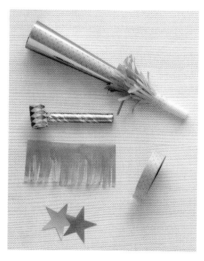

FOR HORNS AND NOISEMAKERS Cut a piece of tissue paper into a 2½-inch-wide strip that is long enough to wrap around the horn or noisemaker several times. With a pair of fringe or regular scissors, trim the paper along a long side, stopping a half-inch from the other long side. Wrap around the horn and secure with washi tape. Use a star-shaped punch to form stars from metallic card stock. Affix stars to horns or noisemakers with a glue dot.

FOR CONFETTI BAGS Trim a piece of card stock the same size of the base of your confetti bag. (Since confetti is so light, the card stock placed in the bottom of the cellophane bag will help the bag keep its shape.) Fill the bag with confetti. Fold top of bag over once. Punch two ⅛-inch holes side-by-side in the top of the bag. Lace a piece of raffia (or thin ribbon or twine) through the holes to secure the bag. Run the ribbon through a metal-rimmed paper tag, wrap it around the noisemaker to attach to top of the bag, and tie a bow to secure.

glittered stirrers

A long, tall drink takes kindly to a sparkling
stirrer. These are easy to assemble, yet just
special enough for a celebration. Dab the pointy
tip of a bamboo skewer with a small amount
of white craft glue. Insert that end into a gold
glittered pom-pom (available at crafts stores).
Let dry completely.

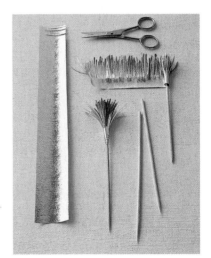

starburst swizzle sticks

Create fireworks long before midnight arrives with celestial swizzle sticks, made from wooden skewers rolled in metallic paper fringe.

WHAT YOU WILL NEED Lightweight metallic wrapping paper, scissors (or fringe scissors), wooden skewers, double-sided tape

Cut out strips of metallic wrapping paper, 2 inches wide and 12 inches long. Make deep, narrow cuts along one long side of each strip, leaving a ½-inch border. Starting at one end, wrap the bottom of a strip around the top of a wooden skewer (above, right); secure the fringe with double-sided tape. With scissors, trim the skewers to fit the bowl of the glass, plus 1 to 2 inches. Shake each stirrer before using it to fluff the fringe.

paper-cone party favors

The next best thing to ice cream cones? Candy cones! Treat departing guests to individually packaged goodies wrapped up in pretty pearlescent paper, and they can continue to savor the sweetness of the evening the next day.

WHAT YOU WILL NEED Cone clip-art (see page 356), pearlized card stock, craft knife, cutting mat, clear tape or clear adhesive circle labels, scissors, iridescent film, candy, ribbon

Download the clip art and print onto card stock. You'll get four cones per 8½-by-11-inch sheet. Use a craft knife and cutting mat to cut each sheet into quarters. Lay flat, lengthwise, with message facing down. Roll into a cone shape, with "Enjoy!" centered on the cone, and secure with clear tape or circle labels. Cut iridescent film into 7½-inch squares. Place candies in center, bundle them up, and tie with ribbon. Insert into cones.

bubble favors

Fill transparent plastic spheres
(available at crafts stores) with shredded
cellophane and round hard candies as
favors for your New Year's party revelers.
Attach a small round tag to the top.
Displayed in a large footed glass bowl or
goldfish bowl, the spheres will almost
appear to float. You can customize the
treats to match the palette of your
party, swapping out confetti and candy
in whatever color you choose.

SETTING
THE SCENE

glittered balloons

Adorn the wall over the drinks table with a multitude of balloons tinged with shimmery colored glitter. The effect will leave you—and everyone around you—positively bubbly.

WHAT YOU WILL NEED Iridescent fine glitter (in a few different colors), small bowls, clear 5- and 11-inch balloons, funnel, spoon, balloon pump, removable adhesive hooks

1 Pour glitter into individual bowls, separated by color. Stretch each balloon to make inflation easier. Insert a funnel into the lip of each balloon, and add glitter using a spoon (1 teaspoon for a small balloon; 2 teaspoons for a large balloon). Adjust the amounts of glitter to achieve the desired color and brightness.

2 Using a pump, inflate each balloon. Move the glitter around the balloon by adjusting the angle of the nozzle. (Do not blow up the balloons by mouth, since you'll risk inhaling the glitter.) Knot each balloon. Create an arrangement of balloons on a wall, securing them with adhesive hooks.

new year's party streamers

Leftover holiday wrapping paper gets a fresh start when transformed into party decor. Cut metallic paper into circles to make shimmering streamers that descend from above, mimicking the famous Times Square ball drop. You can also use the same paper to line a set of drink trays. As a final touch, repurpose tiny fluted baking tins into glistening tea-light holders.

WHAT YOU WILL NEED Spray adhesive, card stock, metallic wrapping paper, adjustable circle cutter, hole punch, jump rings (available at crafts stores), monofilament, thumbtacks or removable adhesive hooks, ruler, rimmed serving tray, laminating kit (optional), double-sided tape

FOR CIRCLE STREAMERS Working in a well-ventilated area, attach wrapping paper to each side of the card stock with spray adhesive. Let dry completely. Using the cutter, cut out graduated circles from the covered card stock (those shown are 2 to 3½ inches in diameter). Punch a hole at the top and bottom of every circle except the smallest one (make 1 hole at its top edge). Connect the circles using jump rings (used in jewelry-making), with the largest circle at the top and the smallest at the bottom. Repeat the process to make more streamers, varying the lengths for visual interest. Hang them from the ceiling using monofilament and thumbtacks or adhesive hooks.

FOR TRAY LINERS Measure the interior base of a rimmed serving tray. Cut wrapping paper to fit. If desired, have the paper laminated (at a stationery store or with an at-home kit) for longer wear, cutting the paper slightly smaller to allow the laminated edges to fit the tray. Insert liner into tray and secure it with double-sided tape.

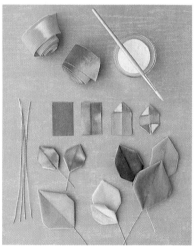

citrus centerpiece

A bright arrangement of glittered faux lemons, piled high with velvet leaves and silver balls,
brings sophisticated cheer to a sit-down celebration, especially on First Night. To wish guests
a sweet New Year, offer a basket of lemon-drop candies at each plate.

WHAT YOU WILL NEED Single-faced velvet ribbon (green and yellow), scissors, iron, white craft glue, white fabric-covered floral wire, clear glitter, bowl, small paintbrush, faux lemons, spoon, small wired silver ball ornaments

To make the velvet leaves, cut rectangles (twice as long as they are wide) from velvet ribbon. Fold one rectangle in half lengthwise (with velvet side facing in). Press with a dry iron. Open the rectangle; lay it velvet-side down. Fold corners to meet at the fold; secure with glue. Lay a piece of floral wire (3 inches longer than leaf) along the fold on the back of the leaf; secure with glue. Repeat, varying folds for leaves of slightly different shapes. To make the glittered lemons, cover your work surface with paper and put glitter in a shallow bowl. With the small paintbrush, coat lemons with glue. Roll lemons in glitter, spooning as needed over the top to distribute the glitter evenly. Shake off excess, and let lemons dry before arranging as a centerpiece; tuck leaves and silver balls among the lemons.

paper-streamer backdrop

Hang honeycomb streamers en masse, and you've got a chic way to decorate a Champagne bar—
or any party focal point that needs more oomph. The key is to layer different varieties (we used
leaf, arcade, and pageant garlands, all available from party supply stores and online) to create a curtainlike
effect. Hang the streamers from the ceiling with masking tape or removable adhesive hooks.

paper-puff ornaments

Party decorations don't need to cost a fortune to look extravagant. These floating ball ornaments are delightfully frilly, but they're made from two commonplace, inexpensive materials: Styrofoam balls and paper cupcake liners. You'll need two or three packages of baking cups for each ball. Estimate 65 mini cups for a 3-inch Styrofoam ball, 95 for a 4-inch ball, and 180 standard-size cups for an 8-inch ball.

WHAT YOU WILL NEED Curved upholstery needle, monofilament, Styrofoam balls (3-inch, 4-inch, and 8-inch), pencil, mini and standard cupcake liners (we used white paper and foil liners), hot-glue gun, wide ribbon, removable adhesive hooks

Use the upholstery needle to thread a length of monofilament into a Styrofoam ball and then out again. Knot the monofilament, creating a loose loop from which to tie a ribbon. Place the eraser end of a pencil in the center of a cupcake liner, and bunch the liner around the pencil. Hot-glue the liner to the ball, pressing with the eraser to help it adhere. Repeat, covering the ball with densely packed paper cups. Hang the ball from the ceiling with a length of ribbon and an adhesive hook. Repeat to make and hang more balls of various sizes and at various heights.

Valentines come in multiple forms and sizes and colors, but nearly every example features a single shape: the heart. This long-acknowledged symbol of love and emotion graces cards and notes and other greetings, and often informs the shape of the offering itself, as in the celebrated Valentine's Day box of chocolates. In this chapter, you will find **TOKENS OF AFFECTION** for all your nearest and dearest; the presents and wrapping ideas include love-knot bracelets, beautiful flower arrangements, doily-detailed gift toppers, and lots of heart-shaped treats for children to hand out to classmates and teachers. From our earliest school years, we learn how to create **LOVE NOTES**: cutout paper hearts carefully inscribed with handwritten messages of love. As adults, we still adore all the flourishes of handmade Valentines—and so we continue to make and give them. We've included lace-edge stationery and sweet sentiments crafted from quilling paper among our crafts projects. Finally, decorating and entertaining touches are grouped together into **HEARTS ON DISPLAY**; each one is easy to put together and guaranteed to help set the stage for a supersweet occasion.

PREVIOUS Doily Gift-Bag Clips, see page 32 for how-to

TOKENS OF AFFECTION

DOILY GIFT TOPPERS The frilly fun of doilies can turn ordinary gift boxes into unabashed expressions of love. Some rose-colored paper and dotted ribbon in the same palette complete the presentation. For the how-to, see page 33.

doily gift-bag clips

It's easy to create a little romance with inexpensive paper doilies. Their characteristic cutwork can double as stencils to transfer charming, nostalgic designs onto paper hearts. Attach clothespins to the backs to create clips that secure simple paper gift bags. The same technique can be used to make Valentine's Day cards or gift wrap.

WHAT YOU WILL NEED Paper doilies (available at supermarkets, crafts stores, and kitchen-supply stores), card stock, paintbrush, gouache (opaque watercolor, in shades of pink and red), pencil, scissors, white craft glue, clothespins, paper gift bags

1 Use the doily as a stencil: Position one on a piece of card stock, and paint over the holes using a brush and gouache in your desired color.

2 Once the paint is dry, remove the doily and draw a heart on the card's painted surface. Cut it out, and glue a clothespin to the back. Let dry.

3 Fill gift bags with candies and other treats, and secure the top of each bag with a finished clip.

doily gift toppers

Paper doilies can seem especially ubiquitous this time of year, but with just a snip here or a fold there, you can transform them into whimsical, butterfly-like Valentines. Or, simply secure a large doily to the top of a gift box with a wide grosgrain ribbon (see bottom gift on page 31 for an example).

WHAT YOU WILL NEED Paper doilies, scissors, gift box, glue stick, thin satin ribbon

To make a three-dimensional butterfly topper, cut smaller medallions from the centers of two paper doilies. Fold the medallions in half, and use a glue stick to affix, with creases adjoined, to the top of a package. Cut small slits at folds and insert thin ribbon, securing at the bottom of the box with glue stick.

four doily gift-wrap ideas

Dress up your Valentine's Day offerings with lacy-looking wraps and vintage-inspired decorative details. Paper doilies can be easily cut to form flowers, medallions, snowflakes, and hearts.

doily garlands

Upgrade simple bags with ribbon or twine woven through the holes of doilies. Embellish small gifts (such as the soap in front) with medallions or stars snipped from larger doilies. Overlap the pieces on a length of thin red ribbon; wrap around the package and secure with double-sided tape. Trim a tall cellophane bag (shown in back) with three medallions threaded with ribbon, evenly aligning them along the front of the bag. Secure with a heart-shaped tag.

dotted details

Customize foil-wrapped chocolate squares with tiny white pieces snipped from larger doilies. Use white craft glue to adhere a piece to each wrapper. The assortment of shapes and colors creates a mosaic almost too stylish to eat.

bejeweled heart-shaped box

Covered in moiré fabric, satin cording, a luxurious pink bow, and faux gemstones, this heart-shaped container takes the box of candy to a new level: It's a treasure all its own. Tuck indulgent sweets inside, or use it to hold a slim volume of poetry, a silk scarf, or another gift for anyone who appreciates a little luxury. The box itself is meant for saving; it can hold sentimental keepsakes long after the holiday is over.

WHAT YOU WILL NEED Ruler, craft knife, 2 pieces of mat board (32 by 40 inches), bejeweled heart-shaped box templates (see page 356), pencil, scissors, hot-glue gun, moiré fabric (about 1 yard; we used a pale apricot), decoupage glue and sealant (such as Mod Podge), foam craft brush, cording on cotton tape (about 2½ yards; we used coral), wire cutters, costume jewelry bracelets or necklaces with faux gemstones, grosgrain ribbon (4 to 5 inches wide, about 1½ yards)

1 Make box: Using a ruler and a craft knife, cut four 32-inch-long strips of mat board: two 1⅛-inch-wide strips (for base) and two 1-inch-wide strips (for lid). Download and print templates for the box base and lid; cut out. Trace each template twice onto mat board; cut out. You'll have two bases and two lids; set one of each aside. Place remaining base on a flat surface. Working in sections and starting at the heart's inner point, affix one end of one strip to base with hot glue. Hold until glue dries, about 20 seconds. Continue gluing until you reach the bottom point. Rest base on its side; trim excess strip carefully so ends match up neatly. Repeat to attach a strip to the other side. Repeat to add strips to one lid piece.

2 Cover sides: Cut a strip of fabric that is ⅛ inch wider than the base's side and long enough to wrap around the side of the box. Working in sections and using decoupage glue and the foam brush, align the edge of fabric with the side's top edge; pat in place and trim overhang. Repeat to cover side of lid in fabric.

3 Add decorative base and lid: Cut two large squares of fabric a few inches larger than heart. Brush the top of second base piece with decoupage glue; press it onto the center of one fabric square. Trim fabric to about 1½ inches around heart. Make snips in the excess fabric; glue the flaps to back of base. Repeat with remaining lid piece and fabric square. Using decoupage glue and foam brush, attach cording tape to the back of both pieces so it runs along the edge; let dry. Hot-glue covered base and lid to the bottom and top of box.

4 Embellish box front: Using wire cutters, snip faux gemstones from jewelry. Hot-glue gems to lid. Tie ribbon into a bow; hot-glue to center of lid.

love-knot bracelets

Knots are symbols of everlasting unity. Two types—the cross knot and the overhand knot (the kind you use before tying shoelaces in a bow)—are showcased in these beautiful bracelets. Use silk cord or velvet ribbon to make the bracelets, and fasten them with mother-of-pearl buttons. To make a card like the one shown, download and print the Victorian hand clip art (see page 356) onto card stock.

WHAT YOU WILL NEED Scissors, 4-mm-wide nylon or silk cord or velvet ribbon, liquid seam sealant, mother-of-pearl buttons, foam board, dressmaker pins, tweezers

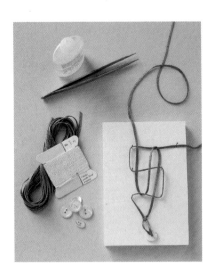

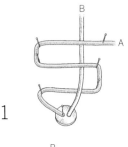

1

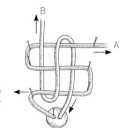

2

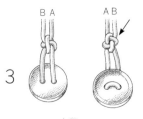

3

4

1 Cut the cord to size (you will need about 45 inches of cord or ribbon for a 7-inch bracelet), and seal ends with seam sealant. Thread through the buttonholes, keeping ends even, and lay button facedown on the foam board. Insert a pin through one buttonhole and cord to secure. Make an S bend with end A (see figure 1), securing by winding around pins; pierce cord with pin at top right corner of S bend. Weave end B over first horizontal segment of S bend, and under the next two.

2 Weave end B back over all three horizontal segments of A, then weave it back down, under the bottom two segments and over the top segment. Remove pins. Using both hands, carefully pull cord as indicated by the arrows in figure 2, making a loose knot.

3 Using tweezers, gently tug up on knot where indicated above and slide knot so it is about 1½ inches from the button. (The back of the knot will resemble the left one in figure 3; the front will resemble the right one in figure 3.) Use tweezers to tighten the knot. Pin it to foam board and secure. Continue adding evenly spaced knots.

4 When bracelet reaches desired length, pinch loose ends together, and tie an overhand knot (figure 4). Trim excess cord; seal ends with seam sealant.

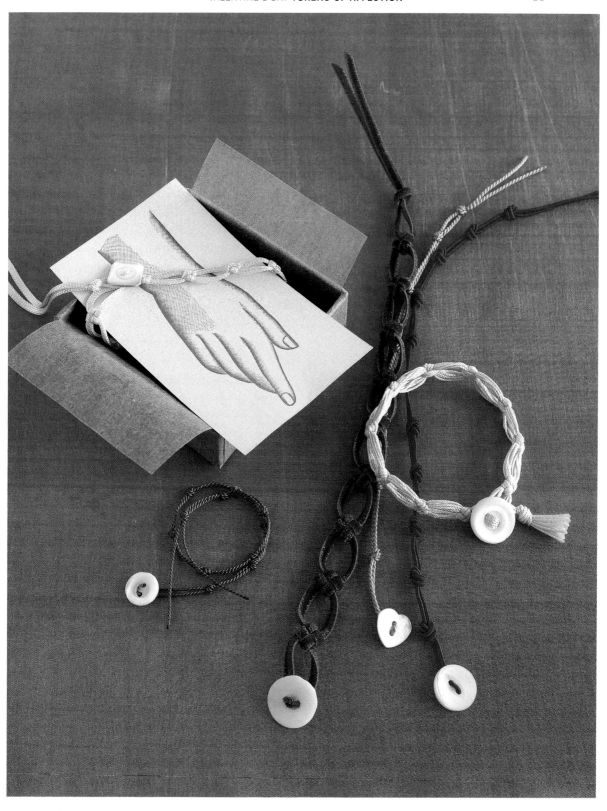

knitted-heart catnip toys

There isn't a kitten in the world that wouldn't purr over a tiny catnip-filled pillow. Our hand-knitted hearts are also stuffed with wool and a jingle bell. This is a great way to use up yarn scraps, since each toy requires less than an ounce. The instructions use standard knitting abbreviations; see the key below. You will need very basic knitting skills to complete the project. For the fundamental techniques, visit marthastewart.com/knitting.

WHAT YOU WILL NEED Yarn (we used chunky weight), size 11 needles (for 3-inch heart; different sizes yield different results), wool stuffing, jingle bell, dried catnip, tapestry needle, scissors

TO KNIT HEARTS Cast on 2 St. Row 1: KFB, K to last St, KFB. Row 2: P. Repeat these 2 rows until there are 14 St (12 rows total). Row 13: K2Tog, K5, and turn work; leave remaining 7 St on needle. Row 14: Working with the 6 St closest to end of needle, P2Tog, P2, P2Tog. Row 15: BO 4 Sts, and trim remaining yarn to 24 inches. Use large needle to weave yarn through back of piece to beginning of reserved 7 St. Row 16: Working with reserved 7 St, K5, K2Tog. Row 17: P2Tog, P2, P2Tog. Row 18: BO 4. Using a large-eyed needle, weave loose ends of yarn into the back of the heart. Repeat knitting instructions above to make a second heart.

TO ASSEMBLE THE PILLOW Stack hearts with right sides out. Using a mattress stitch and a tapestry needle threaded with yarn, sew hearts together along perimeter, leaving a 1-inch gap. Tuck half the stuffing inside heart and insert a bell and some catnip. Add remaining stuffing to fill the heart. Sew closed the 1-inch gap in the heart pillow and weave yarn up inner side of heart. Trim excess yarn at edge of heart so that the loose end is hidden inside.

knitting abbreviations

St Stitch

K Knit

KFB Knit into front and back of stitch (to make two stitches where there was one)

P Purl

K2Tog Knit two stitches together

P2Tog Purl two stitches together

BO Bind off

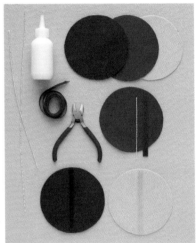

felt "fortune cookies"

Share sweet sentiments—and a few treats as well—with friends and family in these easy-to-assemble felt bundles. After you've shaped the "cookies," cut 4-inch strips from paper, and write a message on each. Slip the fortunes inside the bundles along with small chocolates or other candies.

WHAT YOU WILL NEED Paper or card stock, pencil, scissors, fabric shears, felt (in shades of red and pink), thin ribbon, wire cutters, floral wire, white craft glue

Make a 4½-inch-diameter circle template from paper; trace around a piece of felt and cut out using fabric shears. Cut a piece of matching ribbon slightly shorter than 4½ inches. Using wire cutters, cut a piece of floral wire slightly shorter than the length of ribbon. Affix the wire to the middle of the felt circle with craft glue. Glue ribbon on top, covering the wire. Let dry 30 minutes. Fold the felt circle in half, using the wire as a guide, so ribbon is inside. Next, angle the sides toward each other, bending the wire at its halfway point and forming a fortune-cookie shape. Carefully peel back one flap of the felt cookie, and insert a paper fortune and a few candies. Fold the flap back over to close cookie around contents.

felt button covers

Surprise a child with this no-sew clothing embellishment on Valentine's Day: Cut heart-shaped button covers from pink and red felt pieces (ours are cut from 1-inch squares; you can base yours on the size of the buttons). Fold each in half horizontally and cut a vertical slit, or buttonhole, about the same size as the button. To wear, button up shirt and then slip hearts over buttons.

four easy handmade valentines

Encourage children to show how much they care with cards and goody bags that will outshine any store-bought options. Here are four Valentine ideas guaranteed to delight the recipients. It doesn't take a lot of work—or money—to make any of them. Most require only a bit of cutting and some gluing, and all are easy to personalize.

hand-y valentines

Send a touching message with Valentines traced from little hands. Cut hand tracings from construction paper, then decorate with messages made with rubber stamps, markers, or crayons. Embellish with tiny stickers, sweets, or a toy ring. The finished product will let loved ones know they're the hands-down favorites.

cupcake-paper packages

Fill cupcake liners with an unexpected sweet—candy hearts. Flatten two paper liners. Place one liner faceup and lay the other facedown on top of it. Lift the edge of the top liner and apply white craft glue along a short section. Press to attach; let dry. Continue gluing in sections, leaving the last section open. Fill with candy; seal the opening with glue. Cut out hearts or other shapes from construction paper using a heart-shaped craft punch or scalloping scissors; add a ribbon bow and write a note, as desired. Glue onto center of cupcake liner. Punch evenly spaced hearts along the outer edge.

dotted hearts

Snip a bunch of Valentines for the whole class in a snap.
Cut a heart from a strip of candy dots and glue it to a piece
of construction paper. With scalloping scissors or pinking
shears, cut construction paper to create a decorative border
around the heart. Add a handwritten message or name tag
to the back of each.

paper-bag pouches

Small, flat brown paper bags become extra-special when
they're crafted with care. Use scraps of wrapping paper,
decals, ribbons, and rubber stamps on the front and stuff
the insides with tiny treasures such as candy, mini colored
pencils, erasers, and stickers.

candy and flower arrangement

Flowers and candy are the time-honored touchstones of courtship and romance. But handing over a bouquet or a box of chocolates isn't the only way to show you're sweet on someone—combine the two in one fell swoop. The intense color of tulips such as Red Nova and Pallada coordinate nicely with spicy cinnamon candies; you could also pair pastel-colored flowers with candy hearts in similar hues.

WHAT YOU WILL NEED Two glass nesting vases or containers (such as drinking glasses, one shorter and at least an inch narrower), cinnamon heart candies (about 1½ pounds), 2 dozen red tulips, rubber band, floral or other sharp knife

tips for tulip care

To keep a bunch of tulips looking lovely for as long as you can, start with a very clean vase and fresh water. A tight arrangement will keep them from drooping too much. Use a sharp knife to cut the bottom of the stems at a 45-degree angle so they can drink; recondition the blooms—recutting the stems, changing the water, and adding cut-flower food—every day.

1 Place the smaller vase inside the larger one; if the rims don't align, add candy to the bottom of the outer vase to eliminate the height difference. Fill the gap between vases with cinnamon hearts. Fill the small vase halfway with water.

2 Strip off any leaves that will fall below the water line (to prevent rotting). Secure the stems of a tight bunch of flowers with a rubber band; trim evenly with the floral knife. Set the bouquet inside the smaller vase. Add more water if necessary. Properly cared for (see box, right), the arrangement should last 5 to 7 days.

use Marsh mellow

Maybe 3 packets

, 2 pasta bottles

, 1 smell vase?

heart-and-lollipop flowers

A paper heart is only the start—kids can take this traditional symbol of love and turn it into clever new forms. Here, colorful construction-paper hearts flourish as the petals of a new flower variety—one with a lollipop center.

WHAT YOU WILL NEED Card stock, construction paper, pencil, scissors, hole punch, white craft glue, wrapped lollipops

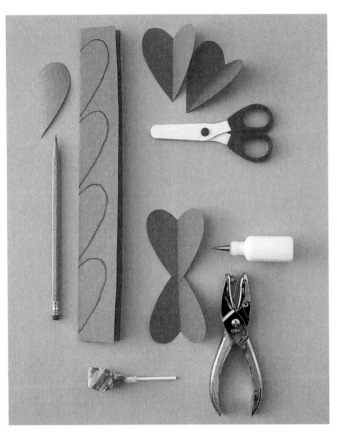

1 Use card stock to make a half-heart template about 3 inches high and 1¼ inches wide.

2 Fold a 12-by-3½-inch strip of construction paper in half vertically, and trace four half hearts along the fold. Cut out hearts; unfold.

3 Stack hearts; punch a hole ¼ inch from bottom. Position petals to form a flower, making sure holes line up. Secure by applying glue around holes; let dry.

4 Write the recipient's name on one of the petals. Insert a lollipop in each.

lace print cards and tags

For anyone who enjoys putting sweet nothings in writing, a set of stationery adorned with painted frills makes a truly heartwarming gift. Tuck a set inside a blush-colored box for giving—and keep a few extra sheets for your own correspondence. Lace, paper, and ink are almost the only supplies you need. Practice this technique a few times on scrap paper before printing directly on stationery, gift tags, or envelopes.

WHAT YOU WILL NEED Lace trim, scissors, kraft paper, sheet of glass (from a picture frame, or custom cut at a hardware store), painter's tape, 2 brayers, water-based block-printing ink, toothpicks, colored stationery (paper, envelopes, and gift tags), paper towels

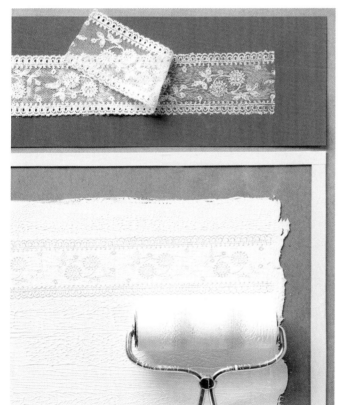

1 Trim the lace 1 inch longer than the item to be printed to ensure clean edges. Cover your work surface with kraft paper to avoid any unwanted ink smudges.

2 Make sure your sheet of glass is large enough to accommodate the lace you will use. Tape the edges of the glass to prevent cuts. Using a brayer, spread a thin, even layer of ink on the glass. Place the lace with the side to be printed facedown on the ink (the front of the lace often has more relief and will make a more detailed print). Firmly run the brayer over the lace once or twice. Thin lace should be completely saturated.

3 Use a toothpick to lift a corner of the lace. With your fingertips, peel the lace from the glass. Lay one end of the lace just off the colored paper, and carefully place the rest down. Put a paper towel on top of the lace and roll firmly once or twice with a second, clean brayer; be careful not to shift the lace underneath.

4 Peel off the lace using the toothpick. Let paint dry. You can wash and dry the lace and reuse it to print if desired.

folding heart valentine

A pretty paper heart, folded to form an envelope, can be more than just a greeting: It's also a clever package for tiny surprises, such as a pair of concert tickets, a simple piece of jewelry, or a few candies. Origami paper is best for this project because it folds easily and crisply. Other papers can be used, as long as they aren't too heavy or stiff. Also consider double-sided papers, since both sides will be visible.

WHAT YOU WILL NEED Folding heart template (see page 356), origami or other decorative paper, scissors, pencil, bone folder, ruler, ribbon (optional)

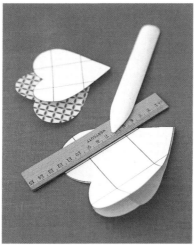

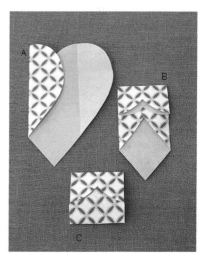

1 Download and print the heart template; if necessary, enlarge it so that the square in the center is large enough to fit whatever you want to tuck inside (these envelopes work best for flat objects). Cut out. Trace the outline of the template onto decorative paper with a pencil. Cut out just inside the pencil outlines to avoid having to erase them later.

2 Laying the template over the cut-out heart, lightly fold the paper and make creases along the four lines with the bone folder and the ruler. Set creases with the bone folder. Remove template. Write greetings inside the heart, as desired, and place small flat objects in the center before proceeding to fold.

3 Fold in each side of the heart (A), then fold down the top (B), smoothing each crease with the bone folder or your finger. Slip the point of the heart into the open top (C), making sure that it fits snugly before completing the fold. If you want to seal the packet with a bow, make slits wide enough to accommodate a piece of narrow ribbon in the top and bottom creases of the square. Multiple hearts can be nested, as long as each fits within the center square of another when folded.

"rose"-printed stationery

Some leafy vegetables make sumptuous floral-shaped stamps. Here, the cut end of a head of Treviso radicchio yields a beautiful roselike print. You can vary the stamp shapes by using other leafy vegetables, such as romaine lettuce stems or brussels sprouts cut in half.

WHAT YOU WILL NEED Treviso radicchio (available at greengrocers and some supermarkets), sharp knife, large stamp pad, cards or other stationery, paper towels

Cut off the stem end of the radicchio with a sharp knife and stand stem on a paper towel, cut side down, for 5 minutes to dry. Press cut side onto the stamp pad, then onto the cards or stationery, blotting on a paper towel between presses. Let dry completely before inscribing card.

fingerprint stamps

Tiny red and pink hearts formed from two impressions of an ink-stained finger are truly one of a kind. Requiring little more than blank tags and a nontoxic stamp pad, this is a perfect Valentine project for kids. They should be able to cross off their list of classroom pals in no time.

crayon and waxed-paper hearts

Filling a window with waxed-paper hearts makes a wonderful craft activity for a wintery day—and helps spread the Valentine's Day sentiment. You probably have all the supplies you need for this kid-friendly project (you can even put all those broken crayons to good use). Spend a couple of hours making these hanging Valentines, and in return, the bright sunbeams of winter will color the room with romance.

WHAT YOU WILL NEED Waxed paper, crayons, handheld pencil sharpener, kraft paper, iron, needle, silk thread

1 Begin with a 12-by-16-inch sheet of waxed paper. Fold it in half along its length; unfold. Deposit wax-crayon shavings (made with the pencil sharpener) evenly, but not thickly, across one half of the paper.

2 Fold the clean half of the waxed paper over the shavings. Crimp the three open edges with a ½-inch fold to hold in the shavings.

3 Protect your ironing surface with kraft paper. Place the waxed paper on the kraft paper, and cover it with another sheet of kraft paper. Iron lightly on medium heat, checking after every few passes. Stop when all the shavings have melted. Let cool.

4 Trace and cut out hearts of various sizes. Using a needle, string each heart with silk thread for hanging.

tissue-paper heart chains

With just a few folds and a simple cut here and there, everyday napkins are transformed into charming tabletop decorations—perfect for a Valentine's Day tea party.

WHAT YOU WILL NEED Square paper napkins (pink and red, in various sizes), paper scissors

1 Position a prefolded square paper napkin so that the closed corner faces you. Fold right corner toward left corner and flatten, forming a triangle. Fold left corner toward triangle's longest side and flatten, forming a narrower triangle (A).

2 Using scissors, cut a convex arc from triangle to create top of half a heart (B). Cut off bottom of triangle from left to right (C) to create lower heart half, leaving at least ¼ inch intact on right edge of heart half. (Left side of triangle will be center of heart.)

3 Unfold (D). Repeat with napkins in several colors and sizes.

Signs of rebirth are everywhere you look in the springtime. Outside, plants are sprouting from the thawing earth, nearly ready to explode into vibrant life. Inside, we set our minds to crafting and decorating for Easter, a holiday closely associated with new beginnings. Easter activities and domestic pursuits honor the promise of the season: dyeing eggs and arranging them in woven baskets; finding the perfect bunch of delicate blooms for a center-piece; fashioning tiny replicas of vegetables and leaves as reminders of the reawakened garden. To that end, we've included our best ideas for giving a warm, cheerful welcome to spring. The personalities and charming details of beloved **BABY CHICKS AND BUNNIES** emerge from simple supplies like yarn, felt, colored paper, and pipe cleaners. **EGGS BY THE DOZEN** offers a primer on dyeing, and step-by-step instructions for a host of techniques, including marbleizing, decoupage, and wax-resist designs. Note cards, table decorations, and favor bags with flower, butterfly, or other nature motifs commemorate the wonderfully recurring **SIGNS OF SPRING**.

PREVIOUS Fuzzy Baby Chicks and Pipe-Cleaner Baskets, see pages 70 and 71 for how-tos

BABY CHICKS AND BUNNIES

BIG-EARED BUNNY This little bunny has a body made from a pink-dyed egg, and facial details—ears and teeth—cut from felt. His feet are also cut from felt (see template, page 356), and his nose is a mini pom-pom. For his whiskers, twist short lengths of embroidery floss and glue in place. Cut a hole in the center of his feet to keep his body standing up. To make the carrots that fill the basket, cut leaves from green crepe paper, bunch them, and glue to the top of orange-dyed eggs.

fuzzy baby chicks

Spring is the softest of seasons, a time of downy-feathered friends in mellow pastel hues. You can create Easter decorations in similarly gentle colors and textures— like tiny pom-pom creatures in pipe-cleaner baskets (see opposite for basket how-to). Such a display is bound to bring out the tender side in just about anyone who sees it.

WHAT YOU WILL NEED Bumpy pipe cleaners, fabric dye (such as yellow, blue, pink, purple, and green), scissors, tweezers, white ½-inch pom-poms, fabric glue, pink or orange paper, black embroidery floss, small colored feathers

Dye bumpy pipe cleaners (see note, right). Each chick requires one pipe cleaner with 4 bumps (A). Snip one bump off each end of the stem (B). Using tweezers, tightly roll 1 bump into a spiral, leaving the skinny end straight (this will be the chick's head). Repeat with the other single bump; then flatten the spiral some-what between your fingers to form the chick's tail section. For the body: Trim the skinny ends from the remaining section of pipe cleaner (2 bumps joined by a skinny section). Using the tweezers, roll each bump toward the center into a tight spiral; stop just before the skinny part. Bend the skinny portion between the bumps to form a W shape (C). Turn both spirals so their flat sides are facing. Wire the chick's head and tail pieces to the W portion of the body piece using their skinny ends. Insert a ½-inch pom-pom between the 2 body spirals to form the breast (D); secure with glue. For the beak: Fold a piece of pink or orange paper in half, and cut out a small triangle (E); affix it with glue. For each eye: Make a knot from 4 strands of embroidery floss; cut any excess thread from the knot (F). Attach eyes with glue. For the tail: Trim off the tip of a small colored feather, and glue it to chick's tail end (G).

dyeing pipe cleaners

Although pipe cleaners and bumpy pipe cleaners are available in a variety of bold colors, we dyed white ones to achieve a pastel palette. Buy white pipe cleaners and bumpy pipe cleaners, and yellow, purple, blue, pink, and green fabric dye. Dilute three tablespoons of each dye with 2 cups hot water; for the latter three colors, mix in varying amounts of yellow to achieve desired hues (you may need to experiment a bit). Follow manufacturer's instructions to dye the stems; let dry overnight.

pipe-cleaner baskets

Small baskets are perfect to hold tiny baby chicks, chocolate eggs, and other candies. Use them as ornaments to decorate an Easter feather tree or set one at each place setting as a favor for brunch or dinner guests.

WHAT YOU WILL NEED Pipe cleaners, fabric dye (optional, see note opposite; such as yellow, blue, pink, purple, and green), scissors, large Styrofoam egg, straight pin, clear fabric glue

Each small basket (about 2½ inches in diameter) requires 5 pipe cleaners. Dye the pipe cleaners (see note, opposite). Cut 4 pipe cleaners in half and twist them together at their midpoint to create a star shape with 8 spokes. Add a ninth spoke by hooking the end of another pipe cleaner to the star's center (A). Trim the ends so all the spokes are the same length. Space the spokes evenly apart. Hook the end of another pipe cleaner to one of the spokes, near the star's center. Center the bottom of the Styrofoam egg over the star, and pin it to secure. Curl the spokes upward to form a cup shape (B). Begin tightly weaving the pipe cleaner over and under each of the spokes. When you reach a pipe cleaner's end, wire another to its end, and continue weaving; repeat until you reach the ends of the spokes. Lock in the weave by hooking each spoke end over the last pipe cleaner. For the basket handle: Twist 2 pipe cleaners together; trim them to the desired length (C), and hook them onto the lip of the basket. To make the base: Twist 2 pipe cleaners together to form an appropriate-size circle; trim any excess (D). Attach the circle to the bottom of the basket with glue. To make larger baskets, up to 4 inches in diameter: Follow the same technique, but use full-length pipe cleaners for the star instead of halves.

pom-pom bunnies and thread-wrapped carrots

Entice Peter Cottontail and his pals out of hiding with some strategically placed carrot ornaments, plucked fresh from your crafts table. Once you've captured the palm-size creatures, place them in a child's Easter basket or use them as decorations all over the house. The bunnies are so easy to assemble, you can produce a whole family of them in an hour or two.

WHAT YOU WILL NEED White pom-poms (you will need 1-, ¾-, and ⅜-inch sizes for each bunny), clear fabric glue, pom-pom bunny feet and ear templates (see page 356), felt (in pink and white for bunnies, and green for carrot tops), scissors, embroidery floss (in black and pink), polymer clay, perle cotton thread (in peach and bright orange), screw eyes (optional)

FOR BUNNIES Connect the 2 larger pom-poms with fabric glue; let dry. Download and print the templates. Using the templates as a guide, cut 2 ear shapes from pink felt and the feet from white felt. At the narrow end of each ear, apply a dab of glue, and pinch the end together to seal; set aside to dry. For each eye, make a knot from 4 strands of black embroidery floss. To make the nose: Use your fingers to coat several inches of pink embroidery floss with fabric glue (to stiffen it). When the glue dries, snip 2 small pieces of the floss, and glue them together in an X shape. Use dabs of glue to attach the eyes, ears, nose, tail, and feet to body. Let dry.

FOR CARROTS Form carrot shapes out of polymer clay (ours range from 2½ to 4 inches); bake them according to the manufacturer's instructions. To make hanging carrots (to use as ornaments for a feather tree), insert screw eyes into tops as clay cools. Using the technique for thread-wrapping an egg described on page 101, wrap the forms in the perle cotton thread, starting from the top and working down. Cut small strips from green felt, and glue them to the wide end of each carrot to simulate tops.

bunny garland, cupcake flags, and favor bags

Charming bunny-shaped paper decorations multiply quickly, thanks to their no-fuss construction. String them into a garland that hangs over the dessert table, attach them to wooden skewers to make flags for cupcakes, or trace their shape to form "windows" in jelly bean–filled favor bags. A simple recurring theme such as this helps unify any holiday display.

WHAT YOU WILL NEED Bunny templates (see page 356), pencil, colored vellum (in pastel shades such as pink, purple, blue, and green), craft knife, hole punch, yarn, cellophane bags (2½ by 1 by 6 inch), jelly beans or other small candies, thin ribbon, bamboo skewers, glue stick, magazines (for drying)

FOR GARLAND Download and print the upright bunny template. Trace the shape onto vellum and cut out with a craft knife. Punch 2 holes in each rabbit's head; thread with yarn. Repeat to add more bunnies, spacing evenly, until you reach desired length.

FOR FAVOR BAGS Cut an 11-by-2½-inch strip of colored vellum. Position the upright bunny template so its ears fall 2½ inches below the top edge of the strip. Trace the shape and cut it out with a craft knife. Fill cellophane bags with candy, stopping about 2½ inches from the top. Wrap vellum around each bag, fold the top edges together, and punch 2 holes through the folds. Thread a length of ribbon through the holes, and tie.

FOR CUPCAKE FLAGS Trace either template (sitting or upright bunny) onto vellum and cut out shapes (you will need two for each topper). Cut bamboo skewers into 6-inch lengths. Coat the back of 1 rabbit and the top ½ inch of a skewer with a glue stick. Sandwich the stick between 2 matching rabbits. Dry the skewered bunny between the pages of a magazine for 30 minutes.

see-through easter "baskets"

Clear glass jars show off chocolate bunnies and other Easter candies to their best advantage, and they make fun, modern alternatives to traditional woven-basket candy containers. Retro sweets such as Holland mints, pillow candies, and jelly beans give the jars a dose of old-fashioned candy-shop appeal. Tie a ribbon around a chocolate bunny and nestle it on a bed of paper "grass," surrounded by candy eggs. Or simply fill a jar with bulk candy, alternating types to create solid-colored stripes. Wrap ribbon and a gift tag around jar lid, securing with double-sided tape.

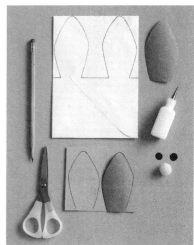

envelope bunny treat bags

If you're hosting an Easter celebration, make it an especially hippity-hoppity one by providing bunny-shaped bags filled with sweets. Easily crafted from envelopes and construction paper, these come together in minutes.

WHAT YOU WILL NEED 5¼-by-7¼-inch envelopes (in white or pink), envelope bunny template (optional; see page 356), scissors, construction paper (in black and pink), white craft glue, regular and colored pencils, small pom-poms (in white or pink), candy

Seal the flap of an envelope and draw bunny ears aligned with the long edge, as shown (download and print the template and trace, or draw freehand). Cut along the outline through both layers of the envelope. Use black construction paper rounds to make eyes and pink paper for ears (by tracing template or drawing freehand); glue details to the front of the envelope. Glue on a pom-pom nose; use a colored pencil to draw the bunny's mouth. Fill envelope with candy.

springtime daffodil basket

Set in a rustic boat-shaped birch basket, this cheerful yellow landscape feels like a bright, sunny day. The moss and soil (both inside a plastic liner) are contoured for a more realistic look, and two types of daffodils (Small Talk and Tête-à-Tête) are removed from pots in smaller clusters to make the flowers appear to be growing naturally.

WHAT YOU WILL NEED Plastic basket liner, birch basket, potting soil, potted daffodils, clump moss (available online and at florist-supply shops), 1⅛-inch pom-pom maker (available at crafts stores), thin yellow mohair yarn, scissors, yellow twine, needle and yellow thread, orange pipe cleaners, white craft glue, orange felt, black embroidery thread

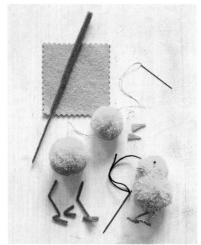

FOR BASKET Place plastic liner inside the basket and fill with soil so that it is mounded in spots, like a hilly field. Turn daffodils out of their plastic pots and plant in soil; for a more natural look, carefully tease apart daffodils before planting. Place the moss on top. Plant additional daffodils between the moss seams and in the soil to fill in any bare spots. Set the basket in a sunny location and water frequently so it will last for several weeks.

FOR CHICKS Following the instructions on page 342, make a 1⅛-inch pom-pom with yellow mohair; use yellow twine to tie the yarn in the middle before removing plastic pieces. Trim to make it round, if necessary. To make a smaller pom-pom for the head, use less yarn or trim down a larger pom-pom. To connect the head and body, sew the pom-poms through the centers with yellow thread. For the legs, trim the nap from the pipe cleaners. Cut two 2½-inch pieces, and bend them in the middle for "knees." Notch the legs at the bottoms (as shown above). Bend a ¾-inch piece of pipe cleaner

into a V, dab glue on the point, and cinch inside notch to create feet. Put a dab of glue on the top of the legs and push into pom-pom so that chick will be able to stand; adjust position of legs and allow glue to dry with chick standing up. Cut two tiny triangles of felt for the beak and adhere with dabs of glue. Thread a needle with black embroidery thread and tie a knot at the end. Insert the needle where an eye would be and push it through the head, leaving the knot flush with the pom-pom surface; knot and trim the other end to form a second eye. Place chicks on top of moss in basket.

EGGS BY THE DOZEN

egg-dyeing techniques: the basics

Dyeing and decorating eggs is the quintessential Easter craft. Following a few basic steps will help ensure a successful batch every time. Nearly all of our egg-dyeing techniques can be used on hard-cooked eggs, but if you want to keep your eggs year after year, blow them out before you begin.

BLOWING OUT EGGS To empty a raw egg, begin by using the tip of a craft knife to pierce small holes in both ends of the egg; turn the knife in one of the holes to widen it slightly. Then, poke a straightened paper clip through the larger hole to pierce and "stir" the yolk. Hold the egg, larger hole down, over a bowl, and blow the contents out with an aspirator (available at drugstores). Rinse the shell well and let dry.

DYEING EGGS Protect your work surface with paper towels or newspaper. In a heatproof bowl, cup, or jar deep enough to let you submerge an egg completely, mix 1 teaspoon of vinegar and 20 drops of liquid food coloring (use more to intensify color, if desired) with 1 cup of hot water. To create different tints of a color, vary dipping times: Submerge eggs for less than 1 to 3 minutes for light colors, or leave in for as long as 10 minutes for deeper shades. Using tongs makes handling the eggs easier. To make a two-color egg, dye the whole egg first in a light color and let the egg dry for 15 minutes. Then, in a shallow container, submerge just half of the egg into a darker color.

MAKING A PIN-BOARD Made with pins and foam board, this rack helps eggs dry evenly after dyeing and minimizes the mess. Use ½-inch-thick foam board cut into a 10-inch square (or make it as big or as small as you want). Using a pencil and ruler, draw a grid. Where the lines cross, insert pins. Set dyed eggs on pins to dry.

egg-dyeing techniques: wax-resist patterns

Melted wax can be applied to eggs in all sorts of creative designs before they are dyed. The waxed areas won't absorb color, creating patterns in relief. Start with room-temperature eggs (if they're cold, the wax won't adhere).

DRAWING WITH A CRAYON For simple motifs, use a crayon. To create a design, draw on a white, brown, or dyed egg with any color (the crayon color doesn't matter because you will be removing the markings), then submerge egg in dye until desired color is achieved. Remove from dye and let dry, about 10 minutes. To remove wax, place eggs on aluminum foil on a rimmed baking sheet in an oven preheated to 250°F. When wax starts to melt (after about 10 minutes), it will glisten and shine; remove eggs from oven and hold in a paper towel as you wipe off the wax.

DIPPING Start with a white egg, or one dyed a solid color. Melt beeswax in a double boiler. Dip both ends of egg in hot wax to coat, leaving a wide stripe of eggshell uncoated in between. Submerge egg in a dye bath until desired color is achieved. Blot egg with a paper towel, and dry it on a pin-board, about 10 minutes. Dip egg ends in wax again, deeper this time, leaving a narrower uncoated stripe in the center. Submerge egg in another dye bath, until desired color is achieved. Remove egg, blot, and dry on pin-board. Remove wax as directed (see left).

WRITING WITH A STYLUS For more intricate designs, use a stylus, a penlike tool with a barrel at the end for dispensing wax. You'll also need a candle, a beeswax patty, and paper towels. Heat the barrel of an empty stylus by holding it near a lighted candle. Scrape the beeswax to fill the stylus, then heat the barrel again near the flame. Touch the tip of the stylus to the egg, letting wax come out, and draw your design. Heat and refill the tool as necessary. Make line drawings, or fill in areas if you wish. Let wax dry, then submerge egg completely in dye until desired color is achieved. Remove egg; let dry on a pin-board, about 10 minutes. Remove wax as directed (see above, left).

egg-dyeing techniques: masked designs

To make more fanciful designs—including stripes, plaids, dots, and other playful patterns, adhere common supplies such as tape or stickers to eggs. After you dye the eggs and remove the "masks," the designs stand out.

PLAID EGGS

1 Start with a plain or pale-dyed egg. Wrap ⅛-inch strips of masking tape lengthwise around the egg for stripes; rub the tape edges with your fingernail to get a good seal. Submerge egg in dye bath until desired color is achieved. Remove, and blot with a paper towel. Let dry on a pinboard, about 10 minutes.

2 Make crosswise stripes around the egg using ¼-inch masking tape. Rub down tape; dye egg in a darker color and dry as before. Remove tape.

OTHER MASKING MATERIALS

For a variety of design options, use the same process as for plaid eggs, but with rubber bands or small stickers. (Dots, stars, and ring-shaped paper reinforcers from the office-supply store all work well; big stickers are less likely to lie flat on the rounded surfaces of an egg). For an example of this technique using cut and punched vinyl, see page 94.

naturally dyed eggs

The custom of dyeing eggs each spring takes us back to medieval times, when people made "pace" eggs using natural dyes to celebrate the season and Pasch (the original name given to Easter or Passover). Though synthetic dyes are much more commonly used these days, you can still color eggs the old-fashioned way, using natural items you may already have in your kitchen—such as coffee, cabbage, berries, and spices. This technique works best with white eggs; use a cold- or hot-dipping method depending on how intense a color you desire.

WHAT YOU WILL NEED Eggs (use hard-boiled eggs for cold-dipping and raw eggs for hot-dipping), white vinegar, pot, natural dye ingredients (such as onion skins, coffee, berries, cabbage, beets, or turmeric; see chart, right), pin-board (see page 81)

color chart

▨ **CHARTREUSE** Boil eggs with 3 tablespoons of turmeric, then cold-dye in red cabbage.

▨ **SIENNA** Boil four packed cups of onion skins (from about 12 onions) in the water, or wrap and secure individual skins with twine around each egg.

▨ **LIGHT PINK** Boil a 12-ounce package of cranberries; use as a hot or cold dye.

▨ **RICH BROWN** Boil eggs in 1 quart of coffee.

▨ **DARKER PINK** Use 4 cups of chopped beets.

▨ **LAVENDER** Use 4 cups of frozen or fresh blueberries.

▨ **GOLD** Use 3 tablespoons of turmeric.

▨ **ROYAL BLUE** Use 2 heads (16 cups) of coarsely chopped red cabbage, 2 additional quarts of water (3 quarts total), and 6 additional tablespoons of white vinegar (8 total); soak overnight for a deeper blue.

For cold-dipping, boil the eggs and ingredients separately. Dip the eggs in cooled, strained dye (see chart) for 5 to 10 minutes and dry them on a pin-board. The color will be subtle, translucent, and—unless the eggs were rotated vigilantly—somewhat uneven.

To get richer, more uniform color, boil the eggs with the natural dyeing ingredients (also known as hot-dipping): Use 2 tablespoons of white vinegar per quart of water. Place eggs in a pot; cover with 1 inch of water. Add natural dye ingredients (see chart), bring to a rolling boil, then reduce heat and simmer, 20 to 30 minutes. Rinse with lukewarm water and let dry on a pin-board.

botanical-patterned eggs

Tiny, delicate sprouts of greenery and herbs announce the arrival of spring. How fitting, then, that they should adorn a batch of colored eggs. The practice is centuries old—in the Middle Ages, when Easter eggs were often embellished with gold, those who couldn't afford such extravagance made do with leaves and flowers.

WHAT YOU WILL NEED Egg white, small bowl, eggs (blown-out or hard-boiled), tiny paintbrush, herb sprigs (such as flat-leaf parsley, thyme, oregano, cilantro, and dill) and small leaves, tweezers, nylon stocking, scissors, string, vinegar, egg-dyeing solution, spoon, bowl or pan, paper towels, aspirator (if using blown-out eggs), pin-board (see page 81)

1 Place egg white in a small bowl. With the paintbrush, apply egg white to the back of a leaf or sprig; use tweezers to center it on an egg, and press down gently with fingers till item is flat.

2 Cut the stocking into 4-inch squares. Lay the egg in the center of the square and pull nylon around it, stretching it taut; tie with string to secure.

3 Make a dye solution, following instructions on page 81. Holding the string, dunk the egg into the dye; press down with a spoon to immerse it completely. Let the egg sit for 5 to 10 minutes, periodically turning and spooning dye over it.

4 Remove egg from dye and blot dry with a paper towel. Snip the string and unwrap stocking to check the color. If the egg isn't dark enough, retie nylon and return to dye. When desired color is reached, remove nylon and carefully peel away the leaf. Blot with paper towels. If using blown-out eggs, blow out any excess water with an aspirator, and place egg leaf-side up on a pin-board to dry completely.

silhouette decoupage eggs

Captured in profile, the iconic images of Easter take on a new sophistication. Use the templates and the simple cut-out silhouette instructions provided to make a whole bunch. Or, save time by cutting out other seasonal shapes with craft punches.

WHAT YOU WILL NEED Blown-out eggs, egg-dyeing solution, white or colored paper (no thicker than construction paper), transfer paper, silhouette decoupage templates (see page 356), tape, ballpoint pen, small scissors, decorative craft punches (optional), decoupage glue and sealant (such as Mod Podge), small and medium paintbrushes, pin-board (see page 81), ⅛-inch-wide silk ribbon, long needle

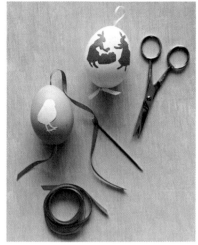

1 Dye blown-out eggs (see instructions on page 81) as desired. Let dry. Lay a sheet of colored or white paper faceup on a work surface. Lay a sheet of transfer paper facedown on top. Download and print the templates. Place on top of the transfer paper and secure with bits of tape; trace the outline with a ballpoint pen. Cut the silhouette along the transferred outline using small scissors. (Alternatively, cut shapes from paper using craft punches.) Coat the back of a cutout with decoupage glue using a small paintbrush. Apply the cutout to an egg; smooth it out with the tip of the brush handle. Let dry. Repeat,

adding cutouts as desired. Apply sealant to the entire egg with a medium paintbrush. Let dry on a pin-board.

2 To create a loop for hanging, thread a 10-inch length of ribbon through the needle. Insert the needle in the bottom hole of the blown-out eggshell; draw it up through the top hole. Leave a hanging loop at the top and draw the needle back down through both holes. Knot the ribbon 2 or 3 times at the bottom (to be sure it can't slip through the hole). Trim the ribbon ends.

marbleized eggs

If the Earth hatched from a giant egg, as the ancient Persians believed, it might have resembled one of the members of this dreamy dozen. Creating the abstract, intricate swirls of color—earthy brown twisting over baby blue, soft beige afloat on buttery yellow— is easier than it looks; the trick is adding oil to the dye. Every Easter egg you decorate this way will be one of a kind, and all are sure to be enchanting.

WHAT YOU WILL NEED Eggs (blown-out or hard-boiled), several mixing bowls (deep and shallow), egg-dyeing solution, measuring spoons, olive oil, fork, paper towels, pin-board (see page 81)

1 Dye eggs in a deep bowl to achieve desired pale shade according to instructions on page 81, and let dry.

2 In a wide, shallow bowl, prepare a second batch of dye in a darker shade or a different color than the base color (use a ratio of 15 to 20 drops of food coloring to 1 cup warm water and 1 tablespoon vinegar); this will be used to form the swirls. Liquid should be ½ inch deep. Add 1 tablespoon olive oil. Run a fork through this mixture, creating curlicues and breaking up the oil into drops and swirls on the surface.

3 As the oil swirls, place a dyed egg in the mixture and roll it around the bowl to pick up oil streaks; remove the egg.

4 Gently pat the egg with a paper towel. Let it dry, preferably on the pinboard. You can experiment with color combinations, varying the base tints and the swirls to achieve striking contrasts, subtle shadings, or multihued richness.

paper-napkin decoupage eggs

For a bright, fresh look with no dyeing required, apply stylized patterns cut from paper napkins to plain white eggs. Cutting out the shapes doesn't have to be meticulous; a loose trim around the designs will do, as the napkins' white edges will blend into the eggshells. Add coordinating tags to bentwood baskets, then pile in the eggs along with some holiday sweets.

WHAT YOU WILL NEED White paper napkins with printed designs, small scissors, blown-out eggs (see page 81), small and medium paintbrushes, decoupage glue and sealant (such as Mod Podge), pin-board (see page 81), white paper gift tags, ⅜-inch-wide reed (available at crafts stores), oval bentwood boxes, white craft glue, clothespins, decorative ribbon (we used green gingham)

FOR EGGS Trim loosely around the designs on a napkin using small scissors. Separate printed top layer; discard lower sheets. Using a small paintbrush, coat part of an egg with sealant. Apply 1 cutout design to the egg; smooth with the small paintbrush. Let dry. Repeat, adding more designs as desired. Apply sealant with a medium paintbrush to entire egg. Let dry, preferably on the pin-board.

FOR GIFT TAGS Follow napkin-trimming instructions above. Using a small paint-brush, coat part of a tag with sealant. Apply 1 cutout design to the tag; smooth with the small paintbrush. Let dry. Repeat, adding more designs as desired. Apply sealant with medium paintbrush to entire tag. Let dry.

FOR WOODEN BASKET Cut an 8-inch length of reed. Glue strip inside opposite sides of a bentwood box. Secure strip at each end with clothespins. Let dry, then remove pins. Tie gift tags to basket handles with short lengths of ribbon.

vinyl masked eggs

Easter eggs have always been a vibrant bunch, thanks to good old food coloring and a little imagination. These examples take the palette and pattern a step further. The trick? Stickers and stencils that you make from adhesive vinyl sheets and electrical tape. After you apply stick-on shapes to the egg, dip it into dye or dab color right onto the shell. Then repeat, layering on more colors and designs. The technique is charming and easy enough to do with kids, who are sure to love the eye-popping patterns.

WHAT YOU WILL NEED Blown-out eggs (see page 81), adhesive vinyl sheets, scissors, craft punches, egg-dyeing solution (see page 81), paper towels, pin-board, ¼-inch-wide electrical tape, liquid food coloring (for animal stencils, do not dilute), cotton swab, craft knife, fine-tipped permanent ink marker

FOR PUNCHED SHAPES Make vinyl cutouts (such as squares, leaves, or flowers), with a craft punch and apply to an egg. Submerge egg in a dye bath (following instructions on page 81) until desired shade is achieved. Blot egg with paper towel and let dry on a pin-board. Peel off cutouts. Apply a second layer of cutouts (in the same or a different shape). Submerge egg in a different colored dye bath until the desired shade is achieved. Dry egg again. Peel off cutouts to reveal finished egg.

FOR SPIRALS AND SQUARE CUTOUTS Wrap a strip of the electrical tape around an egg. Submerge egg in a dye bath until desired shade is achieved. Blot egg with paper towel and let dry on a pin-board. Peel off tape. Apply a second, same-size piece of tape, wrapping it in the opposite direction. Submerge egg in a different colored dye bath until desired shade is achieved. Dry egg again. Peel off tape.

FOR ANIMAL STENCILS Apply vinyl stencils to a pale dyed egg (for body, use a 1-inch circle punch; bunny ears are made using a ¾-inch punch and a strip of vinyl; baby bird wings are made with half a ¾-inch circle). Using a cotton swab, dab undiluted dye inside the stencils. Peel off stencils. Let dry. Apply two more stencils (for the face, use a ¾-inch circle punch; for the bunny tail, use a ½-inch punch). Dab dye. Peel off stencils to reveal the shape. Make eye stencils using a ⅛-inch hole punch. Dab dye. Cut triangle stencil for nose or beak using a craft knife. Dab dye. Draw a curved mouth with the marker.

CRACKED-EDGE EGGS The two-tone orange and purple eggs on this page get their jagged edges from electrical tape: Use a craft knife to cut a random zigzag pattern into a strip of vinyl electrical tape and position it around an egg that has been dyed a pale color. Dip the egg partially into the same dye bath again, up to the tape, holding it in until the desired darker shade is achieved.

heat-embossed eggs

Rubber stamping, a favorite craft technique, can be far more versatile than just ink on paper. Small stamps can be used on eggs as well and, with the aid of an embossing tool, can create intricate raised designs. Embossing powder hardens into a shiny finish that resists dye, leaving white shapes on colored eggs. Personalize the eggs for place settings, as shown, or arrange a bunch with stamped motifs in a basket as a centerpiece.

WHAT YOU WILL NEED Small rubber stamps, clear embossing pad, eggs (blown-out or hard-boiled), small bowl, plastic spoon, clear embossing powder, pin-board (see page 81), heat embosser, egg-dyeing solution (see page 81)

1 Press a small rubber stamp into the embossing pad, then onto the surface of an egg. The clear adhesive is hard to see, so start with just one or two designs and add more later if desired.

2 Working over a small bowl, use the spoon to sprinkle clear embossing powder over the stamped adhesive; then carefully blow the excess back into the bowl.

3 Place egg on the pin-board. Hold the embosser over the design to melt the embossing powder until it is shiny and solid. Repeat steps 1 through 3 to add more designs to the same egg.

4 Submerge the egg in a strong dye bath for 30 seconds at most; a longer dip may loosen the embossed design. Set egg on pin-board and let dry completely.

fanciful egg gift boxes

*Made from German cardboard boxes, glittered and embellished Easter eggs are
perfect for hiding tiny presents, such as the vintage Steiff bluebird shown opposite.
You can use the same technique to decorate blown-out eggs, but sturdy cardboard
is the best choice if you want to start a lasting family tradition.*

WHAT YOU WILL NEED Cardboard egg gift boxes (available online), acrylic paints (in blue and
white), white craft glue, small dish, painter's tape, paintbrushes, paper plate, spoon, fine-
glass and shard glitters, paper or silk millinery leaves or flowers and trim (available at specialty
trim shops and online), paper borders, construction paper, basket, vintage velvet leaves

FOR GLITTERED EGGS Paint egg boxes
with blue acrylic and let dry. Pour
some glue into a dish, and add about
a teaspoon of water to thin out. Cover
the lip of an egg box with painter's
tape to prevent glitter from sticking.
Paint the outside of an entire egg half
with the glue wash. Working over a
paper plate, sprinkle the egg surface
with spoonfuls of glitter—try using
fine-glass glitter on some eggs and
shard glitter on others. Lift egg to
shake off excess, and reapply what is
on the paper plate until egg is completely coated. Repeat with other half.
Let dry 30 minutes.

FOR EMBELLISHMENTS Using the same
glue-glitter technique, add sparkle to
the leaves and flowers. Decorate edge of
eggs (above lip) by gluing on vintage-
style paper borders. Glue flowers onto
egg either singly or clustered in a
pattern. If desired, tuck construction-
paper tags behind a flower or leaf, or
glue them in place.

FOR GRAY-WASHED BASKET Mix a dab
each of blue and white acrylic paints
with 4 ounces of water. Brush it on
the inside of the basket to test color;
adjust if necessary with more blue,
white, or water. Paint entire basket with
wash and let dry. Twist velvet leaves
around the handle.

thread-wrapped eggs

Tradition may call for Easter eggs to be hidden, but oversize handcrafted specimens like these are too pretty to tuck away. They're made of Styrofoam wrapped with lustrous perle cotton thread and decorative trim, and then displayed on a mantelpiece. Among the eggs are a mix of fresh and faux spring blossoms: indigo grape hyacinths, lavender lilies of the valley, and creamy daffodils mingle with iridescent velvet millinery flowers, all arranged in sterling silver egg cups and julep cups.

WHAT YOU WILL NEED Styrofoam eggs (those shown are 4 to 5½ inches tall), T-pins, small paintbrush, white craft glue, perle cotton thread (a type of embroidery floss), scissors, fabric millinery flowers and other trims (available at specialty trim shops and online), clear fabric glue

1 To wrap an egg, first insert a T-pin at one end of an egg, then brush a small area surrounding the pin with craft glue. Hook one end of the thread around the pin, leaving a ½-inch tail; adhere the tail to the glued portion of the egg. Carefully begin wrapping the thread in a single layer around the pin and over the tail end, adhering it to the egg. After covering the glued portion with thread, use a paintbrush to apply glue to another small section; continue wrapping. Repeat until half of egg is wrapped; snip thread. Remove pin and repeat process on other end until entire egg is covered. Fill in any gaps with more thread.

2 To add trimmings and fabric millinery flowers, simply choose accents in complementary colors, and use the fabric glue to adhere them. To replicate the eggs pictured opposite, tie a single ribbon horizontally around an egg's midpoint, or wrap decorative trim vertically at evenly spaced intervals; secure trim in place with fabric glue.

papier-mâché eggs

Papier-mâché, the grade-school art class favorite, can turn strips of paper into sophisticated oversize eggs, ready to be cracked open and filled with treats. Each egg has three layers of paper: one for the shell, one for the lining, and a third in between. Experiment with different materials, such as plain newsprint, metallic gift wrap, or tissue paper, and try using contrasting colors for the inner and outer shells to add an element of surprise. Eggs in a variety of sizes make for a more interesting display. To make the pom-pom chicks shown opposite, see page 78.

WHAT YOU WILL NEED Assorted papers (such as newsprint, gift wrap, and/or tissue), metal ruler, balloons, glass bowls, decoupage glue and sealant (such as Mod Podge), scissors, pencil, craft knife, white craft glue

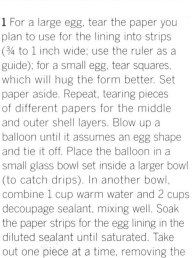

1 For a large egg, tear the paper you plan to use for the lining into strips (¾ to 1 inch wide; use the ruler as a guide); for a small egg, tear squares, which will hug the form better. Set paper aside. Repeat, tearing pieces of different papers for the middle and outer shell layers. Blow up a balloon until it assumes an egg shape and tie it off. Place the balloon in a small glass bowl set inside a larger bowl (to catch drips). In another bowl, combine 1 cup warm water and 2 cups decoupage sealant, mixing well. Soak the paper strips for the egg lining in the diluted sealant until saturated. Take out one piece at a time, removing the excess liquid with fingers. Working from the top of the balloon to the bottom, apply the pieces, overlapping slightly, to cover completely. Add middle and outer shell layers while paper is wet; mix up more sealant as needed. Next, reinforce the top and bottom of the egg by crisscrossing shorter strips of outer-shell paper. Let the egg dry for at least 24 hours, keeping it away from heat, which can cause buckling.

2 Re-adhere any unglued bits of paper or trim them with small, sharp scissors. With a pencil, mark a jagged line all the way around the upper part of the egg. Using a craft knife, slowly cut along the line (this will pop the balloon); if the egg dents, push it back out from the inside. To make a pedestal, cut the egg close to the top; glue the upturned cap to the bottom of the egg; let dry.

3 When displayed on their own, the "cracked" tops showcase the colored paper linings inside. Use them as dishes for foil-wrapped chocolates and candy eggs.

SIGNS OF
SPRING

birch basket with spring flowers

This oversize nest cradles an exuberant mix of blooms from spring-flowering bulbs—the botanical counterpart to newly hatched chicks. Pliable birch branches circle an ordinary woven basket, giving the nest its ethereal appearance.

WHAT YOU WILL NEED Birch branches (available at florist-supply stores), wire cutters, round woven basket, 24-gauge brown wire, floral foam, plastic liner, tulips and daffodils

1 Gather a bundle of birch branches. Cut off the fine tips, then cut the branches into varying lengths (6 to 12 inches).

2 Using the wire, secure the end of a branch to the base of the basket. Bend the branch along the basket's curve, wiring every 4 or 5 inches so that loose ends stick out. Repeat with remaining branches, overlapping them to conceal the basket.

3 Cover the bottom of the basket with plastic liner. Soak the floral foam in water for about 1 hour before using. Set foam in liner and arrange flowers. For tips about proper tulip care, see page 47.

flowery notes

Since everything else is blooming at this time of year, why shouldn't your personal correspondence blossom, too? Convert store-bought cards into pop-up stationery or create your own from scratch. Seal envelopes with cut-paper flowers.

WHAT YOU WILL NEED Patterned scrapbook paper, flowery notes template (see page 357), pencil, craft knife, cutting mat, envelopes (large enough to hold cards with flower "open"), glue stick

Trim and fold scrapbook paper to desired card size. Download and print the template, enlarging or reducing it as desired; print and cut out. Unfold the card. Center the template over the middle of the crease; trace half of the flower in pencil on the front of the card. Working on a cutting mat, cut along the pencil mark with a craft knife. For an envelope seal, reduce the template as desired; print and cut out. Trace the flower onto paper; cut out. Adhere the flower to a sealed envelope with a glue stick.

punched-paper envelope clasps

Pretty nature-themed closures make seasonal greetings and gifts more fun to open. Cut flower and leaf shapes from colorful card stock using craft punches (available at crafts stores and stationery suppliers). Sew a pair of fasteners in place with silk beading cord, double-knotted on the back. Then wind a length of cord in a figure eight, or simply wrap it around an envelope or bag, to close.

butterfly basket place cards

Welcome your guests with delicate flights of fancy. Light-as-air butterflies beautifully evoke the freshness of the season; choose fabric or feather versions from a crafts store or preserved butterflies from online nature stores.

WHAT YOU WILL NEED Small wicker baskets, plastic liner, fresh clump moss (available at online florist-supply shops), scissors, white paper, pen, straight pins, artificial or preserved butterflies

Line each wicker basket with plastic. Fill with a mound of clump moss. Cut a narrow banner from white paper and inscribe it with a guest's name. Use a straight pin to affix butterfly and name tag to moss.

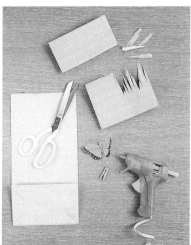

springtime favor bags

Even if it's not quite warm enough for running barefoot, you can evoke an outdoor mood with grass-and-butterfly goody bags, inspired by the wonders of spring.

WHAT YOU WILL NEED Green paper gift bags, scissors, double-sided tape, off-white paper lunch bags (the lunch bags should have the same size base as the gift bags), hot-glue gun, miniature clothespins, fabric butterflies, small favors, paper name tags

Keeping a green bag folded, cut off its top two-thirds. Cut a grass design into the bottom portion of the bag, being careful not to cut the base; unfold. Place double-sided tape on the base of an off-white bag and fit it inside the trimmed green bag. Hot-glue a miniature clothespin to a fabric butterfly (remove the wire if necessary); let dry. Fill the bag with favors and fold down the top edge. Pin the butterfly and a name tag to the top. Repeat to make more bags.

crepe paper carrots

Made of wrapped paper, these little lifelike bundles offer a new twist on an old-fashioned craft, the crepe-paper surprise ball. When you unwind the paper, you find trinkets inside—such as jewelry, small novelties, or tiny toys. Whip up a basketful and customize them for guests of any age. Display them as a centerpiece or leave them by the door as a take-home token.

WHAT YOU WILL NEED Crepe paper streamers (in shades of orange and yellow), assorted trinkets, green crepe paper sheet, crepe paper carrot leaf template (see page 357), pencil, scissors, hot-glue gun

Loosely wrap crepe paper streamer to form a carrot shape, making it thicker at the top and thinner at the bottom. Tuck in gifts as you work. Press the end of the paper down into the top. Download and print leaf template and cut out. Fold green crepe paper in half against the grain. Trace template onto folded paper. Cut out leaves, unfold, and bunch at the bottom. Tuck leaves into carrot top and secure with a dab of hot glue.

tulip and candy table setting

Give the Easter table a big burst of color with woven baskets filled with French tulips interspersed with dishes of jelly beans in coordinating colors; when closed, the flowers resemble brightly dyed eggs. Place a plastic liner inside a basket. Press clumps of wheatgrass, with a bit of soil still attached, around the edges of the liner. Place a second, slightly smaller liner inside the first liner to hold the wheatgrass in place. Pour water into plastic liner. Cut tulip stems about 2 inches long and nestle them in the center of the basket.

She's still got that potholder you made in second grade tucked away somewhere. She's a mother, after all, and every trinket you give her instantly becomes a precious memento. On this very special occasion, pull out all the stops and make pampering Mother your number one priority: Hand-stitch a greeting card rather than simply writing one; create dreamy sea-glass jewelry (and beautiful velvet-covered boxes to keep it in); and put together sumptuous floral arrangements and fragrant sachets. Gifts for Mom are all about saying "thank you" in the most personal and unforgettable ways you can think of. No matter what gift you choose for Mom, a handcrafted note will help reinforce the sentiment. We provide instructions and inspiration for lovely **KEEPSAKE CARDS**, with exquisite details, family photographs, and carefully folded bits of colored paper that open into surprising and delightful pop-up flowers. Gift ideas include **LITTLE LUXURIES**, filled with handmade presents that any mother is bound to appreciate, and, of course, **BOUQUETS AND BLOOMS**, featuring pretty ways to present bunches of blossoms to Mom on her holiday.

PREVIOUS Button-Embellished Cards, see page 116 for how-to

KEEPSAKE CARDS

HAND-EMBROIDERED BOTANICAL CARDS
A handmade card like this one will live in Mom's keepsake box for many years. Soft colors and vintage-inspired details stitched in gold make these cards appear especially out-of-the-ordinary. For how-to instructions, see page 117.

button-embellished cards

Make a sweet button sampler as a Mother's Day card, stitching shimmering bouquets of mother-of-pearl or pretty plastic buttons. This is a great way to showcase distinctive buttons from a vintage collection or to use up any extras from the bottom of your sewing box. Vintage buttons can also be found at flea markets and online auction sites.

WHAT YOU WILL NEED Scissors, white and colored card stock, pencil, needle, thread or embroidery floss, buttons, thin ribbon, double-sided tape

1 Cut out card stock to desired sizes: Cut smaller pieces to be embroidered and slightly larger pieces in contrasting colors for the backings.

2 With a pencil, lightly mark placement of buttons onto the top piece of card stock, and sketch design for leaves and other details. Poke holes along the lines with a needle.

3 Using thread or a single strand of embroidery floss, embroider lines with a running stitch, passing the needles through existing holes, or make French knot details (see pages 344 and 345 for basic embroidery instructions). Use thread to attach buttons (reinforce with glue if you like).

4 Add a ribbon (see page 112 for placement), threaded through two holes, and tie in a bow.

5 When you are satisfied with your design, attach embroidered card to backing with double-sided tape.

hand-embroidered botanical cards

Inspired by cards from the 1920s, these layered floral greetings begin with clip art (we offer both black-and-white and color versions of the clip art). You can play with the palette and embellish the images as much or as little as you like, using watercolors to paint the flowers and leaves and gold thread to stitch the stems and tendrils (the tiniest blossoms are made with French knots). Leaving more white space on the card gives it a modern effect.

WHAT YOU WILL NEED Embroidered card clip art (see page 357), ivory card stock, watercolor paint and paintbrush (optional), embroidery needle, metallic gold thread, tented card, double-sided tape

1 Download and print clip art onto ivory card stock, scaling to desired size. Paint the card details with watercolor if desired; let dry completely.

2 With an embroidery needle, poke spaces (³⁄₁₆ inch apart) along the thin black lines of the stems, flourishes, or letters.

3 Thread two 24-inch lengths of gold thread through the needle (use more strands if you prefer a thicker gold line). Knot the 4 ends together. Trim excess thread close to knot (to keep the back of the card stock neat).

4 The stems and flourishes are made using a backstitch (see pages 344 and 345 for basic embroidery instructions). Continue in this pattern until finished. After the last stitch, knot on the back of the card stock and trim excess thread close to knot. (Rethread needle as needed until you finish embroidering the design.)

5 To create the centers of the flowers, embroider French knots (see basic instructions on page 345). For larger knots, wrap thread more than two times.

6 Cut embroidered card stock to fit on tented card, and mount using double-sided tape.

GREETING

HORIZONTAL FLOWERS

VERTICAL FLOWERS

photo gift topper

When searching for the perfect way to express your heartfelt appreciation, remember that a picture really is worth a thousand words. Scan and print a favorite family image—or multiple images—and use it to decorate a very-well-deserved gift. Wrap a ribbon around the present and affix the ends with double-sided tape. Center the picture over the ribbon and attach with glue stick or double-sided tape.

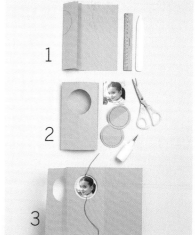

spinning snapshot cards

Skip the greeting-card store and put a more personal spin on your Mother's Day correspondence: Construct a simple folded card and add a photo that twirls on a string. Kids can choose two images to glue back-to-back, or cover the other side of a photo with colorful paper.

WHAT YOU WILL NEED Colored card stock, ruler, scissors, bone folder, photo(s), white craft glue, string

1 Decide on the finished card's size, then cut a sheet of colored card stock to that height and three times the width. Fold the paper width-wise into three equal parts. Unfold, and fold left flap over middle (to form the card's front); using a bone folder, fold both flaps in half. Draw a half circle (or square) over outer fold; cut out, through both layers, just outside line.

2 Trim cutouts. Lay one on photo; trace. Cut out photo; glue onto cutout. Cut out another photo, if using.

3 Glue string between photo and the second cutout (or the second photo). Place string in fold of middle flap; position photo in hole. Glue left flap to middle, trapping string inside. Trim string.

pop-up bouquet card

For moms near and far, this gorgeous greeting card makes for a very special delivery. A flat card pops up into a three-dimensional arrangement that's much less expected than a bouquet of roses. Though it looks intricate, it takes only some snippets of folded paper and cleverly placed double-sided tape to complete.

WHAT YOU WILL NEED Text-weight paper in various colors (we used pinks and oranges, and green for the leaves), petal template (see page 357), pencil, scissors, glue stick, double-sided tape, colored card stock, colored pen, envelope

1 Cut seven 4-inch squares of paper in desired colors. Fold a square into quarters. Fold down one flap diagonally; flip the square of paper over and fold down the other flap, forming a triangle. Download and print the petal template; trace it onto the triangle and cut out. Unfold, and cut one petal from the flower; close the gap by overlapping the petals on either side and securing with a glue stick. Repeat with the other squares.

2 Attach pieces of double-sided tape to the petals, as indicated by dots shown. Start attaching the flowers to one another: B and C each overlap a petal with A; then D goes on top, completely overlapping A.

3 Attach E and F to the stack to overlap B and C.

4 Attach G to the top, overlapping D. Cut out leaf shapes from green paper, place double-sided tape on the bottom, and attach them to the flowers.

5 Cut a piece of card stock into a 10-by-6-inch rectangle, and fold in half to form a card. Place the folded flower stack inside the opened card as shown. Place a piece of double-sided tape as indicated by the dot; close card, and press firmly to adhere. Open card and repeat, attaching the other side of the flower stack to the inside of the card.

6 Write a message inside the card before folding up and placing in envelope. Once the card is opened, the bouquet will pop up completely.

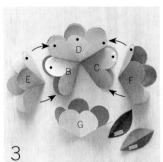

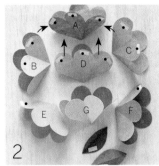

velvet-covered jewelry boxes

If your mother considers accessorizing an art form, she'll appreciate one of these elegant jewelry holders, which evoke the ultrafeminine aesthetics of the Victorian era. Fine millinery flowers and ribbons imprinted with monograms adorn boxes covered in dusty velvets; tucked inside, cleverly pierced ephemera—postcards, snapshots, and vintage playing cards—keep earrings paired and untangled.

WHAT YOU WILL NEED Small screwdriver, hinged wooden box, velvet, ruler, fabric scissors, lay-flat paste (such as Yes! Paste), craft stick, thin ribbon, velvet millinery flowers and leaves (available online and at trim stores), wire cutters, fabric glue (such as Fabri-Tac), wide velvet ribbon (looser piled silk ribbons and silk-rayon blends work best), rubber stamp letters, iron

FOR VELVET-COVERED BOXES

1 With a screwdriver, remove hinges from wooden box. Trace the box bottom in the center of the wrong side of a piece of velvet. Measure the box's depth and add that amount to each side of the drawn rectangle, adding 1 extra inch to each side to overlap box edge. Using fabric scissors, cut out the larger rectangle. Repeat for the box lid.

2 Apply a thin coat of paste to the bottom of the box with craft stick and place it on the rectangle. Turn the box over and smooth the fabric to remove any bubbles. Repeat with the box lid.

Let dry. Apply paste to the sides of the box bottom. Smooth the velvet, leaving flaps at the corners.

3 Carefully trim the extra fabric so the edges abut neatly. Repeat the process for the lid. Let dry. Reattach hinges.

4 Conceal the raw ends of the velvet with ribbon trim: Cut 2 lengths of ribbon equal to the perimeter of the box. Apply paste to the backs of the ribbon pieces. Position the ribbons along the edges of the box bottom and lid, with the ends abutting neatly in back.

5 Compose a pleasing arrangement of velvet flowers and leaves; twist the attached wires together and trim the

wires to a length that can be hidden beneath the petals. Affix to the box lid with the fabric glue.

FOR IMPRINTED VELVET MONOGRAMS

1 Choose velvet ribbon wide enough to accommodate the stamps you're using. Avoid stamps that have intricate patterns or are too shallow. To make a monogram, you can tape three letter stamps together (or have a custom stamp created). Test your materials to determine how much heat, time, and pressure produce the best imprints.

2 To add a monogrammed ribbon to the box lid, cut a length of ribbon the width of the lid, plus the sides. With the steam off, preheat the iron to the cotton or wool setting. Place a rubber stamp, relief side up, on a sturdy, heatproof surface. Place the ribbon, pile side down, over the stamp. Using the part of the iron's soleplate that has no steam holes, press down evenly on the fabric over the stamp. Hold the iron still for 10 to 30 seconds, then lift it straight up. (If the ribbon sticks to the iron, the heat may be too high or the velvet may contain heat-sensitive synthetics.)

3 Gently lift the ribbon (without shifting placement) from the stamp and check if the image is clear. Restamp if necessary. Remove and let cool, then affix to box top with paste or fabric glue.

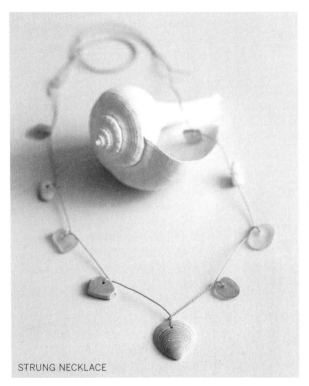

STRUNG NECKLACE

EARRINGS

BRACELET

PENDANT NECKLACE

sea glass jewelry

Gift your mother with a necklace, bracelet, or pair of earrings made of bits of sea glass, shells, and pottery, and she'll be reminded of a favorite vacation spot whenever she wears it. Look for softly wave-worn pieces of glass and ceramic at a nearby beach, or do your searching online (it's not unusual to find bags of the shards in familiar colors for a song on auction sites). With very basic jewelry-making skills and supplies, you can easily transform them into wearable art.

WHAT YOU WILL NEED Sea glass and pottery pieces (an assortment of colors and sizes for a necklace, in the same size and color for earrings or a bracelet; thinner pieces are best for drilling), plastic container, safety glasses, pencil, Dremel craft drill (with #61 diamond bit), silk cord (for strung and pendant necklaces), small clamshell (optional), earring wires, bonding cement (such as Beacon 527), disk-and-loop bracelet form (available at jewelry-supply stores)

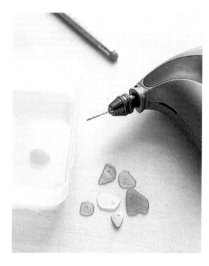 

FOR STRUNG NECKLACE Fill a plastic container with a small amount of water and set a shard of sea glass inside; it should be slightly covered but not submerged (drilling the shard in water will guard against cracking and over-heating). Wearing safety glasses and holding the shard in place with the eraser end of a pencil, make a hole in the glass using the drill fitted with the diamond bit (it may take a few tries to drill through completely). Cut a length of silk cord long enough to fit over your head when looped. String a shard onto the cord and tie with a double knot. Add shards at even intervals. If desired,

attach a small clamshell at the center of the necklace (see opposite, top left). After stringing the last shard, double-knot the cord ends together.

FOR EARRINGS Make holes in pieces as instructed for strung necklace; slip shards onto earring wires.

FOR PENDANT NECKLACE Knot a silk cord around a single, undrilled shard; glue to secure.

FOR BRACELET Apply a dot of bonding cement to each disk on a disk-and-loop bracelet form. Adhere same-size pieces of sea-glass to disks and let dry overnight.

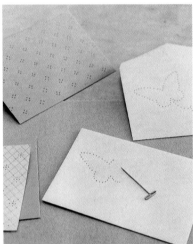

envelope sachets

Not all perfumed envelopes hold love letters. These pretty packets, made especially for Mom, hold scented ingredients and are easy to slip into a drawer or linen closet.

WHAT YOU WILL NEED Envelope sachet templates (see page 357), graph paper (optional), cutting mat or piece of felt, envelope, large T-pin, dried botanicals (combinations such as cedar tips, cedar shavings, and lavender; orange tea and dried roses; or lemon verbena, chamomile, and dried lemon peel), glue stick

Download and print the templates, resizing the design to fit the envelope you're using. Or, make your own pattern; graph paper is perfect for creating a grid design. Working on a cutting mat or piece of felt, lay the template over an envelope, then use a large T-pin to punch holes through the template and both sides of the envelope until the design is complete. Fill the envelope with a combination of dried botanicals; you'll need one to several table-spoons, depending on the envelope's size. With the glue stick, carefully seal the envelope.

handmade botanical soaps

A stack of these sweet-smelling bars is sure to elicit happy summertime memories. Bundle together a few variations (long blades or chopped, clear or white) with waxed paper and twine.

WHAT YOU WILL NEED Five-inch square from a wheatgrass flat, newspaper, flower press (optional), phone book, sharp knife, glycerin soap (clear or white; 1 pound yields 4 to 5 bars), glass measuring cup (or double-boiler), grass fragrance (available at health food stores), 4-inch mini loaf pan, spray bottle with rubbing alcohol, waxed paper, twine

Pull out wheatgrass blades with roots attached. Dry them in a single layer between sheets of newspaper in a flower press or between the pages of a phone book, 2 to 3 days. With a knife, cut soap into cubes; place in measuring cup to fill, then microwave on medium to melt (or use a double-boiler). Stir in a few drops of grass fragrance. For bars with long blades, trim roots from dried grass. Pour a thin layer of glycerin into a mini loaf pan. Lay 5 to 7 blades on top; let dry 30 seconds. Spray with alcohol to eliminate bubbles, and top with more glycerin; spray again. For bars with chopped grass, mix cut dried grass into glycerin and pour into pan; spray with alcohol to eliminate bubbles. Let harden 2 hours. Freeze 20 minutes; release from pan. Wrap stacked bars in waxed paper, and secure the stack with twine.

bath fizzies

Pamper your mother with an old-fashioned kitchen storage jar filled with homemade bath fizzies, in lovely, soothing scents such as grapefruit and eucalyptus. You'll need citric acid, a common food additive, available at wine-making supply stores, some spice shops, and online. When citric acid is combined with baking soda and placed in water, a chemical reaction creates bubbles.

WHAT YOU WILL NEED Citric acid, baking soda, cornstarch, glass measuring cup, fine sieve or flour sifter, organic cane sugar, spray bottle, water, food coloring (about 6 drops), plastic pipette, essential oil (such as grapefruit, eucalyptus, geranium, lemon, tangerine, peppermint, rosemary, or star anise), metal spoon, silicone ice-cube tray, storage jars, tags, thin ribbon

1 Stir together ½ cup citric acid, 1 cup baking soda, and ¾ cup cornstarch in measuring cup. Pass mixture through a fine sieve or a flour sifter into a mixing bowl. Stir in ¼ cup organic sugar.

2 Fill spray bottle with water, and add food coloring. Spritz mixture lightly (it should become damp but not fizzy) until you can pack mixture with your hands.

3 Using pipette, add essential oil, 1 drop at a time, until strength of scent is to your liking (about 10 to 15 drops).

4 Using a metal spoon or your hands, mix ingredients until color is even throughout (mixture will begin to dry out; when this happens, spritz until packable again). Spoon into ice-cube tray, pressing firmly. Let dry at room temperature overnight. Pop out of tray gently.

5 Transfer to jars. Pack each type of fizzy in a separate jar so the scents won't meld. Wrap lip of jar lid with ribbon. Write the name of the scent on a vellum tag (choose a shade that matches the fizzies), and punch a hole in the top. Thread a thin ribbon through the tag and tie around the jar lid.

BOUQUETS AND BLOOMS

everlasting blossoms

Paper flowers mimic the delicate form and rosy hues of cherry blossoms, making them a lovely alternative once the real-life blooms have come and gone. Embellish woody branches that you have pruned from your yard or purchased at a garden center with colorful handmade flowers, and use them to decorate a mantel or table in honor of Mom. Use extra flowers as graceful additions to small gift bags.

WHAT YOU WILL NEED Glassine or vellum (in pink and red), ruler, scissors, branches, vase, pebbles, colored-paper bags, hole punch, coordinating colored brads

FOR FIVE-PETAL BLOSSOMS Cut glassine or vellum into 3½-inch and 4½-inch squares. Fold a square into a flat cone, following figures 1 through 4, right. Using scissors, make 4 angled cuts to remove the top of the cone as shown in figure 5. With scissors, carve out a small rectangular sliver on each side of the cone. Snip off a tiny bit of the pointed tip of the cone and unfold and shape the paper to yield a blossom. Poke the tips of branches through the centers of the blossoms. Place blossom-covered branches in a tall vase filled with pebbles to anchor the display.

FOR GIFT BAGS Fill small colored-paper bags with gifts of your choice and fold down the tops of the bags twice. Punch a hole through one folded corner. Push colored brad through flower, then through hole in the bag to fasten.

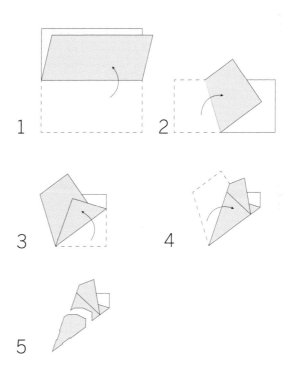

wrapped flower bouquets

A big bunch of blooms from the market makes a fine present for Mom, but if you really want her to feel appreciated, take the time to wrap them right. Creating any one of the wrappings shown here is no more complicated than making a paper airplane or tying a pretty bow, and they all use accessible materials. Each idea is tailored to different flowers—for example, the Ribbon Carrier is great for flowers with sturdy, straight stems, and the corrugated paper of the Buttoned Cone guards against roses' sharp thorns.

ribbon carrier

A broad swath of grosgrain ribbon keeps a bundle of straight-stemmed daffodils as neat as a pin. Select a ribbon or piece of file fabric that is almost as wide as the stems are long, and cut it a few inches longer than the circumference of the bundle. Wrap the ribbon around the stems and pin it to itself along the overlapping edge to secure. To create the handle, cut a 2-foot length of ¾-inch-wide grosgrain ribbon. Tie each end neatly around the wide wrapping, one near the blossoms, the other near the base of the stems.

buttoned cone

To corral a bouquet of roses, cut a sheet of corrugated packing paper and some colored tissue each to about 12 by 18 inches. With an 18-inch length of waxed twine, sew a 1-inch-diameter button to the corrugated paper, halfway down one short side and 2 inches in from the edge; leave a foot of loose twine. Turn the corrugated paper button-side down. Cover with the tissue, leaving an inch of tissue showing at the top edge. Lay the flowers at the end opposite the button and roll them up. Secure by encircling the cone with the twine and wrapping it around the button.

paper envelope

Contain a bunch of fluttery, delicate blooms, such as sweet peas, in a light-as-air wrapper. Start with an 18-inch square of tracing paper.

1 Crease along a diagonal and open.

2 Fold two opposite sides in so that they meet along the diagonal, forming a wedge shape.

3 Fold those edges back on themselves so they align with the long outer edges. Turn the paper over.

4 Fold the outer edges of the wedge in to meet along the center crease. Punch a hole at the tip of the wedge; run a 2-foot length of ribbon through it.

5 Fold that tip back, about one-third of the way up the wedge. Fill with flowers; bring the ribbon around from the back and tie securely.

1

2

3

4

5

iron-on transfer tote

*Iron-on transfers can help create pretty, personal, and practically effortless gifts.
Look beyond the vase this year and give your mother flowers that come to life on
a canvas carryall. Cherry blossoms—a spring favorite—inspired this particular
design; silhouetted in white, they give the solid gray tote a modern screenprinted
look. To apply delicate silhouettes to a colored accessory, you will need transfer
paper that is designed for dark fabrics.*

WHAT YOU WILL NEED Iron-on transfer tote clip art (see page 357), transfer paper (for dark
fabrics), scissors or craft knife, iron, tote bag, pillowcase (to cover work surface)

1 Download and print the clip art onto
transfer paper. Using scissors or a
craft knife, cut out the design, trimming away the outline.

2 Iron the tote bag and the pillowcase.
Lay the pillowcase on a table or other
hard, heat-resistant surface (not
an ironing board, which has too much
padding). Lay the tote bag on top.

3 Remove the paper backings from the
transfers and position the designs
faceup on the bag. Cover with the tissue
paper provided with the transfer paper.

4 With an iron set on high (no steam),
slowly iron on the designs, applying
firm, even pressure (follow the transfer-
paper manufacturer's instructions).
Let cool. Remove the tissue paper.

batik-style table linens

Mom will surely swoon over a new set of floral-patterned table linens, personally created by you. Use fabric markers and stencils to give them the look of patterned Indonesian textiles—with much less effort than the wax-and-dye method of classic batik. You can use our templates or make your own patterns. Choose napkins, place mats, and runners in natural fibers such as cotton and linen, which absorb ink better than synthetics.

WHAT YOU WILL NEED Kraft paper, fabric markers, table linens, batik-style templates (see page 357), waterproof paper, tape, cutting mat, screw punch, craft knife, iron

Cover your work surface with kraft paper. Test a marker on a discreet area of the linen to make sure the ink sets well. Download and print the templates. Lay the template on top of the waterproof paper; tape to cutting mat to secure. Use a screw punch and craft knife to create the stencil. Pressing the stencil edges firmly on the cloth, fill in the design with fabric marker. Repeat to complete the desired pattern. Press using an iron on the appropriate setting for the fabric to set the ink (following the manufacturer's instructions).

custom canvas bag

A cloth bag makes a natural canvas for young artists. This iron-on design, with its coloring-book-style outlines and the start of a sweet sentiment—"Mom, I love you because …"—lets kids create truly one-of-a-kind presents. Download and print the custom canvas bag clip art (see page 357) onto iron-on transfer paper and apply the image to a bag, following the instructions on page 135. Provide permanent markers for coloring and message-writing. Before you begin, cover the table with butcher paper and slip sheets of scrap paper inside the tote to prevent the ink from bleeding onto the other side.

There's no better way to remind Dad of your appreciation than to present him with a gift made with your own two hands. The odds are likely that he won't expect it, but he's sure to be tickled that you went to any trouble. Because every father is unique, we've come up with distinctive and sure-to-please **ONE-OF-A-KIND GIFTS** and some very nice, clever ways to upgrade store-bought ones. Does your dad love to travel? Serve him a drink on a coaster made from a map that will remind him of his last journey or inspire his next. Is he a regular at Poker Night? Make a custom game box with all the necessary accessories and equipment. Or maybe the best thing you can give him is the day off from his chores (our clip-art coupons will fill the bill). Dig into his interests and you'll see that Dad isn't so difficult to delight after all. And just like Mom, Dad deserves a special note on his holiday; we've included several **HANDCRAFTED CARDS** so you can express your love in do-it-yourself style.

PREVIOUS Embellished Game Box, see page 142 for how-to

ONE-OF-A-KIND GIFTS

CLIP-ART FOOD LABELS Our pop-art–inspired labels make it a cinch to turn any of Dad's favorite foods into a custom gift. Download and print the designs (see page 357) onto plain or self-adhesive paper, enlarging or reducing the size as desired. Affix labels to cellophane bags filled with pistachios, jars of homemade pickles and goodies, or store-bought sauces and salsas. Use double-sided tape if you print the labels on plain paper.

embellished game box

He's a pro at gin rummy and he somehow manages to win every hand at poker. Treat Pop with a special box designed to hold playing cards, poker chips, dice, and the all-important score pad. Decked out with paper cutouts of a card suite, this box is easy to assemble, and will be definitely put to good use. You can vary the number of partitions if you want, depending on Dad's interests.

WHAT YOU WILL NEED Wooden hinged box, fine-grit sandpaper, spray paint, ruler, balsa wood sheets (for partitions), thin ribbon, fabric glue, craft knife, white craft glue, paintbrush, card suite template (see page 357), tissue paper, masking tape, cutting mat, heavyweight colored paper, glue stick, game accessories (blank notepad, dice, playing cards, poker chips)

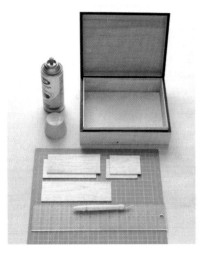

1 Decide how many partitions you want to include (our box has six). Measure the interior of the box to determine the length of each partition. Cut the balsa wood into strips with a craft knife; for accuracy, cut them a little longer than your first measurement, and then trim to fit.

2 To help the paint adhere, first lightly sand the box with fine-grit sandpaper. Working in a well-ventilated area, spray the box and the wood strips with a few coats of paint. Let dry.

3 Use a small paintbrush to coat the edges of each strip with craft glue; affix strips in place.

4 To make a tab, cut a piece of ribbon twice the width of the compartment meant for the cards (this will make it easier to remove the cards). Fold over the edge of one end twice and secure in place with fabric glue. Center the other end along one long side of the compartment, and secure in place with a dot of craft glue. The ribbon should lay flat across the bottom and the other end should extend up the side of the box when the cards are placed in the compartment.

5 Download and print the template. Tape the template on top of a small stack of tissue paper and secure to

a cutting mat with tape. (It is easier to cut a stack of tissue than to cut individual pieces.) Very carefully cut out the shapes with a craft knife.

6 Trim a piece of heavyweight matte paper to the size of the underside of the box lid. Affix tissue-paper shapes to the paper with a glue stick. Let dry. Attach the paper to the lid's underside with glue. Following the instructions for the box lid, decorate the blank notepads with card suite cutouts as well.

embroidered tie

Neckties can seem de rigueur on Father's Day, but they don't have to fly off the store rack and straight into the gift box. Add a bit of personality to the present by embroidering Dad's first or last initial on this year's tie. A simple linen tie makes a good candidate; try embroidery floss in a lighter shade of the same palette for a refined monochromatic look.

WHAT YOU WILL NEED Craft knife, disappearing-ink fabric pen, tie, embroidery floss, needle

Print Dad's initial in a large-size font, then make a stencil of it using a craft knife. Trace the letter onto the tie with the disappearing-ink fabric pen, and embroider a chainstitch with one strand of embroidery floss. For instructions on basic embroidery stitches, including the chainstitch, see pages 344 and 345.

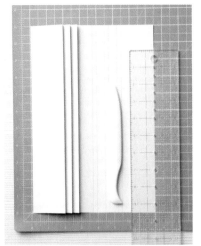

menswear-inspired packaging

The details on these packages resemble those on tuxedo shirts and other men's formalwear, but they are fashioned from folded paper, buttons, and notions. The results look finely tailored and timeless.

WHAT YOU WILL NEED Colored paper, cutting mat, bone folder, double-sided tape, colored wax linen thread, buttons, needle and thread, gray grosgrain ribbon, fabric glue

For tuxedo wrap, place a piece of paper on the mat; starting from the center and making your way out, make a series of evenly spaced accordion folds; crease with the bone folder as you work. Repeat to create folds on opposite side. Affix to package with double-sided tape. Or, thread waxed twine through a row of buttons on a narrow band of paper for a shirtfront look. For tuxedo bow, fold the ends of a piece of ribbon in toward the center, overlapping them; secure with fabric glue. Flatten at center and glue to secure. Cover center with second piece of ribbon placed perpendicular to the first, gluing at back of bow to secure.

button cuff links and card

Fashion a card to look like a dapper shirt cuff, and then use it to present a gift of cuff links made from a pair of shank buttons. This project is easy enough to make for all the dads, uncles, and grandfathers in your life.

WHAT YOU WILL NEED Card stock, scissors, alphabet and punctuation rubber stamps, stamp pad, craft knife, 24-gauge wire, shank buttons, needle-nose pliers

To make the cuff card, cut a 3¼-by-9-inch rectangle from card stock; round the two top corners, as shown. Rubber-stamp greeting on one side. Gently bend paper in half. Using a craft knife, cut slits for cuff links. To make cuff links, hook wire onto a button's shank; secure with pliers. Cut wire to ½ inch; loop through a second button's shank. Repeat.

necktie envelope

The most iconic Father's Day gifts are classic for a reason. Even if your dad doesn't wear a tie every day, there are all kinds of special occasions when he might be called upon to dress sharp. And though one size fits all, you can make your gift feel extra special by presenting it in a handmade fabric envelope that he can use for travel and storage. Sew the satchel from traditional shirting fabric, for a nicely coordinated touch.

WHAT YOU WILL NEED Necktie envelope templates (see page 357), scissors, disappearing-ink fabric pen, two shirting fabrics (one for lining and one for outer fabric, ½ yard each, or 2 old shirts), fabric scissors, sewing machine and sewing supplies, iron, fabric glue (optional), gift tag, thin ribbon, necktie

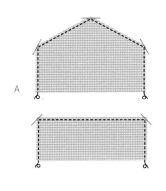

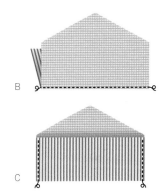

1 Download and print both envelope templates and cut them out: One comes to a point; the other is a long rectangle. Trace each template onto the lining fabric, then onto the outer fabric; cut out all 4 pieces.

2 Match up the shapes, and stack them, right sides facing. Machine-stitch around the pointed set with a ½-inch seam allowance, leaving the long side opposite the point open (figure A, top). Machine-stitch along 3 sides of the rectangular set, leaving 1 long side open (figure A, bottom). Snip off excess fabric from the sewn corners and the top of the point. Turn each pocket right side out and press with iron.

3 Create the envelope: Stack the pockets, aligning the open edges with the outer fabrics facing. Stitch along the open sides only (figure B).

4 Fold the resulting piece at the seam with the lining fabrics facing. Stitch along the 2 short ends from the outside (figure C). (Tip: To create neat, straight seams at the short ends, apply a small amount of fabric glue to the aligned edges before stitching.)

5 To present the gift, cut a length of ribbon and thread one end through the hole of the gift tag. Put a necktie in the envelope. Loop the ribbon around the envelope, and thread the other end up through the hole in the tag. Tie the ends in a knot and trim any excess ribbon.

sock accessory holders

A set of protective pouches should help keep Dad's electronic devices and personal accessories such as cameras, cell phones, and eyeglasses safe and sound. This simple project is great for older children who want to practice their sewing skills. Argyle and striped socks are especially handsome, but you can use any type of pattern or color.

WHAT YOU WILL NEED One adult sock per pouch, disappearing-ink fabric pen, scissors, sewing machine or needle and thread

Turn the sock inside out. The cuff will be the open end of the holder. Lay the device or accessory next to the top of the sock and measure to ½ inch below the bottom (for a seam allowance). Mark a line with the disappearing-ink fabric pen. Cut out with scissors. Machine-sew a seam. Alternatively, you can sew the seam by hand. Turn right side out.

coasters of the world

Map-themed gifts are just right for globe-trotting types. Collect maps from Dad's favorite vacation spots—or from far-flung destinations that he's been dreaming of exploring—and use them to make a set of handy coasters. He'll be inspired every time he reaches for a glass.

WHAT YOU WILL NEED Maps, cutting mat, round cork coasters (available at crafts stores), craft knife, foam brush, decoupage glue and sealant (such as Mod Podge)

Place map on cutting mat, printed side down; then place a cork coaster on top. Cut out circles from the map by tracing around the coaster with a craft knife. Brush sealant onto one side of the coaster, covering it completely. Adhere the back of a map circle to the coaster, smoothing to remove any bubbles. Brush the top and outer edge of the coaster with a thin layer of the sealant and let dry. Repeat to make a whole set.

HANDCRAFTED CARDS

customized coupons

For many fathers, there's nothing better than snagging a great deal. And this booklet is full of 'em: 100 percent off a lawn mowing, car washing, delicious breakfast, or anything else Mom and the kids can think up. Just download and print the designs, make a cover, and then put a whole booklet together.

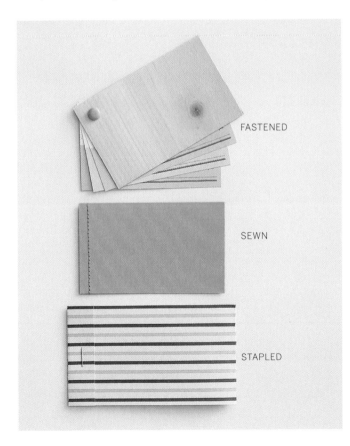

FASTENED

SEWN

STAPLED

Download and print the coupon clip art (see page 357) onto heavyweight matte paper and cut out. To decorate a cover as shown on the opposite page, cut a window in a piece of card stock using a 1¼-inch round craft punch. Bind coupons using one of the following methods:

FOR FASTENED COUPONS Cut colored card stock to the same size as the coupons for a cover; stack it on top of the coupons. With a standard hole punch, make a hole in the upper-left corner of the stack; insert a brad.

FOR SEWN COUPONS Cut a cover from colored card stock and place it on top of the coupons. Secure the stack with paper clips; machine-sew stack together along the left side.

FOR STAPLED COUPONS Cut card stock cover to 2½ by 8½ inches. Fold one end of the strip over by ¾ inch; slide the coupons inside this flap and staple through its center. Bend the opposite end of the cover over the coupons and insert it under the flap (like a matchbook cover); crease the cover at the fold.

jacket lapel card

Here's a fashionable card and gift-holder all in one: a card stock "lapel" complete with a pocket square. Look for a pocket square in a snazzy fabric that your dad will enjoy using, and choose card stock for the lapel in a complementary color.

WHAT YOU WILL NEED Lapel template (see page 357), scissors, colored and white card stock, masking tape, craft knife, cutting mat, bone folder, ruler, double-sided tape, white gel-ink pen, pocket square

Download and print the lapel template, and cut out; tape it onto a sheet of colored card stock on a cutting mat. Cut a ⅛-inch-wide slit for the pocket, following the lines on the template. With the craft knife, cut around the outline of the template. Using a bone folder and ruler, score along the dotted line; remove the template. Flip the card stock over. Fold down the lapel; secure it with double-sided tape. Draw "stitching" along the lapel edges and on the pocket with the gel-ink pen. Write a message below the pocket. Flip the jacket and place double-sided tape along its edges. Flip it again and tape the jacket to the white card stock (as tall as the jacket and twice as wide), folded in half widthwise. Tuck in the pocket square.

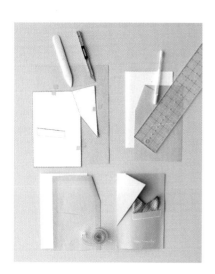

Happy Father's Day!

photo frame card

How can kids spell out their love on Father's Day? By making a card that doubles as a picture frame using the letters of his name (D-A-D). The present will stand proudly on a desk or bureau with the assistance of bent paper clips. Favorite photographs, trimmed to show kids' faces, peek through the holes of the letters.

WHAT YOU WILL NEED Photo frame card template (see page 357), lightweight card stock, scissors, craft knife, photos, clear tape, paper clips, glue stick

Download and print the template directly onto colored card stock. Cut out front and back of frame. Mom can use a craft knife to cut out the middle parts of each letter (don't cut out middle parts of each letter for backing). Trim photos to fit the openings, making them slightly larger than the holes; tape them behind the cutouts. To make the frame stand up, bend open two paper clips and tape the small sides to the backs of the letters at the bottom. Affix the backing to the frame with a glue stick.

folded shirt card

Shirts and ties may be the most traditional gifts for Dad, but a cleverly folded card representing them both feels entirely fresh and new. Choose decorative papers in menswear patterns, such as pinstripes, polka dots, or plaids.

WHAT YOU WILL NEED Decorative papers (8½ by 14 inches each), scissors, glue stick

1 Place paper facedown. Fold in half vertically; unfold. Line up left edge with centerline fold, and crease; repeat with right edge. Unfold, and lay flat.

2 Fold in top-left corner to line up with outermost crease, forming a triangle; repeat on top-right corner. Using index fingers and thumbs, pinch together outside points of each triangle so they meet, and crease.

3 While still pinching triangles, fold down top edge (this will make sleeves).

4 Turn paper upside down, and flip it over. Fold down top edge ¾ inch.

5 Flip paper over. Fold top-left and -right corners so tips meet at center line.

6 Tuck bottom edge under collar, and flatten by creasing.

FOR THE TIE Cut out an 8-by-½-inch strip of decorative paper. Knot strip. Snip close to knot on one end; trim other end to a point. Glue to shirt, just below the collar.

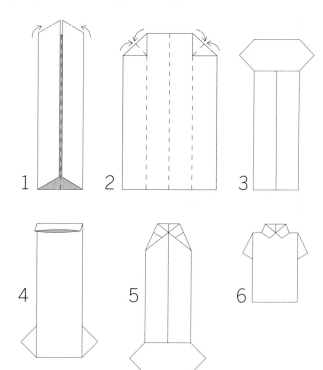

Fourth of July

Independence Day means it's time to display our national pride, and for the crafter, it's also a wonderful opportunity to have some good old patriotic fun. Proudly hail the Star-Spangled Banner and exclaim "Happy Birthday, USA!" The essential tools for a hand-made Fourth of July party are inexpensive and plentiful: paper streamers and fans, lots of bunting, and box after box of sparklers. Outfit the front porch with swags and flags to show your appreciation for Old Glory and host a barbecue with bright, fireworks-inspired table settings. Start and end with the red, white, and blue, and your summer celebration is guaranteed to be especially festive—and memorable. Crafts for this all-American occasion feature an assortment of ideas to show off the **STARS AND STRIPES**, with traditional patriotic fabrics, punched-paper luminaria, and sand-art candles that recall favorite art-class and camp projects. And what would the Fourth be without **FIREWORKS**? Ours are reinterpretations of the real thing, including paper fans stamped with colorful bursts, fun paper pom-pom swizzle sticks, and a clip-art invitation that helps reinforce the dazzling holiday theme.

PREVIOUS Red, White, and Blue Window Swag, Stars and Stripes Medallion, and Flag Fence Swag, see pages 160 to 162 for how-tos

STARS AND STRIPES

BUNTING BANNERS The rocking-chair porch of this house proudly displays patriotic colors. Red, white, and blue bunting is tacked to the eaves of the porch and tied with ribbon at the bottom. Groups of small flags are held up by aluminum brackets.

red, white, and blue window swag

Traditional window swags recall nineteenth-century whistle-stop campaigns. The pieces are easier to assemble than they may appear to be: You just join two pieces of fabric side by side, and then pleat the bottom. We used two styles of cotton bunting for this project and the projects on pages 161 and 162: The window swag and the door medallion use a large stars-and-stripes pattern, while the fence swag uses a classic flag pattern. It's important to machine-stitch the seams slowly using a heavy needle, or stitch by hand.

WHAT YOU WILL NEED Eighteen-inch-wide bunting fabric, rotary cutter or scissors, fusible webbing, iron, sewing machine (optional), disappearing-ink fabric pen, ¼-inch rectangular dowel (3 feet long), ½-inch round dowel (3 feet long), double-sided tape (optional), eye hooks

1 Measure desired length for the flat, non-pleated part of the decoration. Add 30½ inches for the pleated half moon plus 1½ inches for hanging. This is half the length of bunting required for the decoration.

2 Cut 2 identical pieces of bunting: Begin cutting after a star and end right before one, so you'll have about 3 inches of blue on each end. Trim off hems for easier pleating.

3 Join the 2 pieces together side by side (make sure stars line up): Overlap by ½ inch and adhere using fusible webbing; iron to fuse. If you prefer, stitch the ½-inch overlap together. The final width should be about 32 inches.

4 Mark fabric 30½ inches from the bottom edge with the disappearing-ink pen. Pleat the half moon: Starting at the bottom edge, make 1½-inch accordion folds (figure A, right); iron after each fold. Continue up length of fabric, stopping at the mark you made. The raw edge of the fabric should point down.

5 Stitch along the center of the pleated rectangle to create a pivot point (figure B, right). Make one more fold and crease with the iron. Attach rectangular dowel in the crease with fusible webbing; iron, fabric side up. To sew channel at top of swag for hanging, fold fabric over 1½ inches and stitch 1 inch from top edge. Insert round dowel.

6 Fan out sides of the pleated rectangle and adhere with fusible webbing (figure C, right); iron. Or adhere sides with tape for easy disassembly and storage. Screw eye hooks into ends of the round dowel. Hang over a window.

FIGURE A

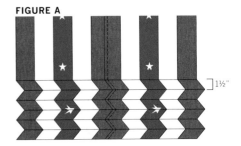

⌐1½"

FIGURE B   REVERSE SIDE

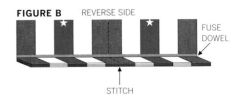

FUSE DOWEL

STITCH

FIGURE C   FRONT SIDE

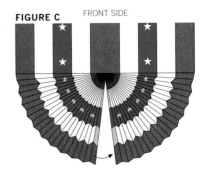

FIGURE D

FIGURE E

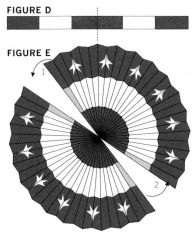

stars and stripes medallion

Round medallions, fashioned from the same bunting as the window swag shown opposite, offer a fresh spin on an American icon.

WHAT YOU WILL NEED Eighteen-inch-wide bunting fabric, ruler, scissors, iron, sewing machine, fusible webbing, double-sided tape (optional), monofilament and needle

Measure two 39-inch-long pieces of bunting. Follow steps 2 and 3 of the window swag how-to (opposite). You now have 1 piece of fabric. Trim off the red and white stripes on both sides, which will result in a 5-stripe pattern: blue, white, red, white, blue. Fold fabric accordion-style in 1½-inch sections (figure A, opposite). Iron after each fold. Continue up length of fabric. Make sure your first and last folds are in the same direction. Stitch along the middle of the folded rectangle to create a pivot point (figure D, left). Connect sides of the rectangle by fanning out fabric from center stitch and adhering with fusible webbing (figure E-1, left); iron. Connect remaining sides with fusible webbing, or tape for easy disassembly (figure E-2, left). Stitch monofilament through the fused edge in the back and hang.

flag fence swag

Along a picket fence, a swag of flags greets Independence Day guests (see photograph, page 156). As with other pleating projects, you should iron the folds in the swag as you go.

WHAT YOU WILL NEED Eight-inch-wide bunting fabric (in flag pattern), ruler, scissors, straight pins, sewing machine

Measure the desired length of your swag. Cut 1¾ times this length of bunting. To pleat the fabric, first lay it down, wrong-side up. To make a single box pleat, crease both edges of a block of blue and fold both creases so they meet in the middle, covering the blue; the red and white stripes will line up (see illustration, right). Iron and pin in place. Repeat along length of fabric. Machine-sew along the top using a straight stitch. Remove pins and flip fabric over. Hang swag with nails or as desired.

REVERSE SIDE

flag centerpiece

Place this easy-to-assemble flag stand—made from a plaque and two finials from a hardware store—on top of a two-tiered cake plate to create a proudly patriotic dessert display for cupcakes, cookies, and other crowd-pleasers.

WHAT YOU WILL NEED Primer, white paint, paintbrushes, wooden finial, 4½-inch wooden plaque, drill, wood glue, circular wooden piece (optional), flags attached to dowels, sandpaper

Prime and paint wooden finial and plaque; let dry. Mark three spots on the base of plaque, evenly spaced and ¼ inch in from the edge. Drill ⅛-inch pilot holes (smaller hole), and then increase the size of the drill bit. (This will make cleaner holes.) Drill holes the diameter of the flag dowels in the wooden base, using the marks as a guide. Drill a hole the diameter of a flag dowel in the same manner on the top of the finial. To attach the finial to the wooden base: Drill a hole in center of plaque slightly smaller than the diameter of the screw (if finial does not have a screw end, attach to plaque with wood glue). A circular wooden piece can be added in the middle for height, if desired. Insert flag dowels into the drilled holes in the base and the finial. If necessary, sand them until they fit snugly in the holes.

outdoor decorating with flags and swags

FLAG UMBRELLA GARLAND AND CHAIR BACKS Dining alfresco on the Fourth of July is a lot more spirited with seating decked out in the grand old flag. For the umbrella (opposite), cut a length of flag garland slightly longer than the perimeter of your umbrella. Measure and mark 7 evenly spaced intervals. Snip nine 10-inch lengths of ½-inch-wide grosgrain ribbon or seam binding; sew ribbons at their midpoints to the garland at each interval and at both ends. Tie ribbons to umbrella spokes. For each chair, tack two ribbons to either side of a single flag and tie to the chair's back. As a finishing touch, coil ribbon around the umbrella pole, affixing at top and bottom with double-sided tape. **HALF-ROUNDS** Festive half-rounds of bunting (above), with grommets for hanging, sway from the beams of a cottage porch; above them, seven flags shoot out from their own flag holders, all attached to a simple plywood plaque (see drilling instructions for Flag Centerpiece, page 163).

star-punched luminaria

Flowery cutouts and a two-tone color scheme render these paper-bag luminarias reminiscent of the starry sky on a midsummer night. Place several of them in the center of a table covered with bandanna-print table linens, and set others along the entry to your party.

WHAT YOU WILL NEED Red and white paper bags, scalloping shears or scissors, decorative craft punches (such as flowers and stars), screw punch, gravel, votive candles and holders

For each luminaria, you'll need a red and a white paper bag of the same size (they can be big or small). Using scalloping shears, trim 1 to 1½ inches from top of white bag. (Or cut a free-form pattern with scissors.) Use decorative craft punches and a screw punch to cut a repeating pattern through bag while it is still folded. Trim ½ inch from top of red bag. Unfold the bags, put the red into the white, and pour in gravel for weight. Place a votive candle inside, checking that the sides of the candleholder extend above the flame, for safety.

striped sand candles

Pay tribute to the stars and stripes (emphasis on the stripes): Dress up candleholders with alternating bands of red, white, and blue sand for table decorations. Designing a sand candle is as simple as pouring layers into a glass.

WHAT YOU WILL NEED Clear drinking glasses, colored sand (red, white, and blue; available at crafts and art-supply stores), clear glass vases or jars, funnel, votive candles

Fill a clear drinking glass with enough sand so that a votive candle placed on top sits just below the rim. Set the glass inside a clear glass vase or jar. With a funnel, fill the gap between the two containers with alternating layers of colored sand, until the sand reaches just below the rim of the drinking glass.

FIREWORKS

magnificent mums

A bunch of inexpensive, spiky spider mums can be tinted to look like sparklers. Working in a well-ventilated area, hold a flower upside down by the stem. Spray the tips with silver or red floral spray, twirling stem in your fingers to coat evenly. Give some blooms a darker coat and go lighter on others. Arrange in vases (the ones shown here are mercury glass). Group blooms of different colors in assorted vessels for a dazzling display.

stamp-art paper fans

In the heat of the summer sun, party guests and parade watchers will appreciate the offer of a paper fan. Ours are hand-stamped with fireworks and other Fourth of July designs. This is a fun and easy project for kids and adults alike.

WHAT YOU WILL NEED White paper fans, rubber stamps (an assortment, including fireworks and stars), ink pads (in red and blue)

Open a fan so that the creases lay flat, and stamp in a random design or create a border along the top. Let ink dry completely before arranging fans in a wicker basket or on a tray. Place on the dining table for a pretty, practical centerpiece, put a fan at each guest's place setting, or simply pass them out as guests arrive.

tissue-paper pendants

Tissue-paper decorations make a breezy addition to a porch or a gazebo for a special occasion. Here, an array of tissue-paper fans, cut to different sizes, creates a fireworks effect. On some of the pendants the center is snipped flat, making room for a patriotic clip-art medallion.

WHAT YOU WILL NEED Honeycomb paper medallions, scissors, tissue-paper pendant medallion clip art (small or large; see page 357), heavyweight paper, scalloping shears (optional), double-sided tape, hot-glue gun, monofilament, removable adhesive hooks

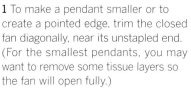

honeycomb basics

These familiar tissue shapes have brightened countless parties and proms, and no wonder: They are inexpensive, easy to store, and instantly impressive. Colors fade with time, lending the accessories a vintage look. Many decorations have loops for hanging. For a floating appearance, use monofilament. Twine or yarn is more visible but can add another element of charm. To hang on walls, use removable adhesive hooks.

1 To make a pendant smaller or to create a pointed edge, trim the closed fan diagonally, near its unstapled end. (For the smallest pendants, you may want to remove some tissue layers so the fan will open fully.)

2 To add a clip-art label, snip the closed fan along one edge of cardboard, cutting off one staple, as shown above on the top left; this will create a flat center. Download and print a clip-art medallion onto heavyweight paper; cut out using scalloping shears. Open fan; secure cardboard edges with double-sided tape. If you cut off a staple to make a flat center, pinch together the loose tissue at center, and secure with hot glue; then hot-glue medallion to center. Hang pendant with monofilament and removable adhesive hooks.

independence day invites

A carefree summer celebration begins and ends with clip-art invitations and party favors. The bright blue card is covered in a pattern of stars and embellished with red-and-white ribbon. Boxes of sparklers, wrapped in clip art–patterned paper, can double as place cards or favors.

WHAT YOU WILL NEED Fourth of July invitation and favor wrap clip art (see page 358), white heavyweight matte paper, scissors, screw or hole punch, ribbon (¼ inch wide), white gel-ink pen, envelopes, craft knife, double-sided tape

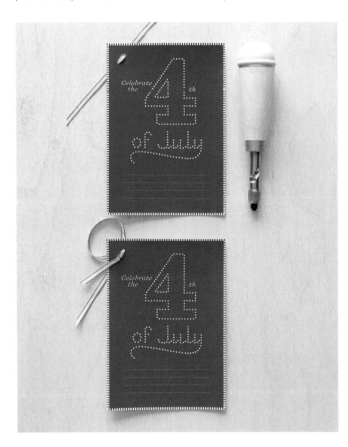

FOR THE INVITATIONS Download and print invitation clip art onto matte paper and trim. Make a pair of holes where indicated on the clip art with a screw or ⅛-inch hole punch (holes must be smaller than the ribbon). Cut two pieces of ribbon 3 inches long. Layer ribbons on top of one another; slip each end into a hole from front. Pull taut; even out ends. Thread each end of ribbon through opposite hole from back; pull taut (left). Trim ends at an angle. Fill out invitation details with the gel-ink pen.

FOR THE SPARKLER WRAPS Download and print fireworks clip art (you may need to adjust size depending on dimensions of sparkler box) onto matte paper and trim. Cut slits along top and bottom of the name label. Thread ribbon through the slits; use double-sided tape underneath to secure. Wrap the box as you would a gift. Write name in label space provided with gel-ink pen.

Celebrate
the

4
th

of July

Picnic at the Parkers'
Saturday, July 4 at 4 pm
14 Bayberry Lane
Charleston, SC 2...

Thomas

Betsy

exuberant table setting

Let fireworks inspire the table decorations on the Fourth of July. Start with napkins, a runner, and place cards in bursts of red, white, and blue, easily created with a bristled kitchen scrub brush. Then add a set of paper pom-poms attached to skewers to bring more bursts of color to the setting. Stick the skewers into sand-filled jars as an alternative to floral centerpieces.

WHAT YOU WILL NEED Kitchen scrub brushes, fabric paint (in red, white, and blue), fabric napkins, fabric place mats or table runner, bottle brush, colored paper place cards, white gel-ink pen, colored vellum, scissors, double-sided tape, bamboo skewers

FOR NAPKINS, RUNNER, AND PLACE CARDS Dip the bristles of a clean kitchen scrub brush into fabric paint. Press bristles firmly onto fabric to create a burst pattern. Repeat to make more bursts, working with one color at a time. Use smaller bottle brushes to create patterns on colored paper place cards, then handwrite each name with a white gel-ink pen.

FOR POM-POMS Fold a 3-by-15-inch piece of vellum in half twice lengthwise. Cut slits every ⅛ inch, leaving ¼ inch at the top uncut. Unfold the paper, and attach a 1-inch piece of double-sided tape to one uncut corner; adhere to a bamboo skewer and wrap the paper around several times. Once you reach the other end, use another piece of double-sided tape to secure. Curl the lower strips with the edge of a scissor blade, as you would a ribbon.

star medallions and gazebo trim

Fabric star medallions brighten up a gazebo dressed with a star-patterned box-pleated trim. Use standard cotton prints for this project—nothing too heavy or light. Spray starch helps the creases keep their shape.

WHAT YOU WILL NEED Cotton printed fabric (in a red, white, and blue palette; about 2½ feet per medallion), heavy spray starch, iron, sewing machine, scissors or rotary cutter, fusible webbing, strong double-sided tape (optional), ¼-inch-wide ribbon, 12-inch-high roll of flag-pattern bunting, straight pins, wide pale-blue grosgrain ribbon, nails (optional)

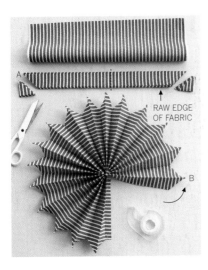

FOR MEDALLIONS Cut a length of fabric: The width will be the diameter of the medallion; the length should be 1.6 times the width (for example, for a 15½-inch medallion, cut about 25 inches of fabric). Follow the fold and stitch steps of the door medallion how-to (see page 161), with one exception: After each fold, spray with starch, and iron. Trim both ends of the pleated rectangle at a 45-degree angle, so the angles slope toward the raw edge of the fabric (figure A)—these cuts create the medallion's starlike points (figure B). Follow the connect step of the door medallion how-to

(see page 161), with one exception: Sandwich a piece of ribbon (it should be long enough to hang the medallion) between the fusible webbing and the fabric.

FOR GAZEBO TRIM Measure the desired length for the trim. Roll out the bunting to a length that's about two times that measurement; cut. Trim the bottom 4 stripes (red, white, red, white) along entire length of bunting. Pleat the fabric: First, lay the fabric down, wrong side up so that the blue blocks of stars run along the bottom. To make a single box pleat, crease both edges of a red-and-white block

(where the stripes meet the blue block), and then fold both creases so they meet in the middle, covering the stripes; essentially, you're matching blocks of blue to blocks of blue (see Flag Fence Swag illustration on page 162 for reference). Pin in place. At the same time, pin the ribbon in place, covering the top two stripes. Repeat along length of fabric. Sew along the top of the panel, through the ribbon and pleats, using a straight stitch. Remove pins. Hang with nails or as desired.

HALLOWEEN

It's Halloween, and creatures of all sorts are on the loose. What was that bump? A knock at the door, perhaps, or something altogether spookier? Let your imagination run free when crafting for this holiday: Carve expressions of ghoulish delight onto pumpkins; dress your home in tatters and spiderwebs; fill paper pouches with goodies and set them out for the taking—and don't forget to include a few tricks along with the treats. Your visitors, innocent and wicked alike, will be frightfully glad they stopped in. All Hallow's Eve, of course, is all about jack-o'-lanterns—you'll see many such examples as well as a primer on the best carving tools and basic techniques in **PUMPKINS GALORE**. To get your home into a properly sinister spirit, we've included spooky decorating projects, such as glittered skulls and bones, in **HAUNTING THE HOUSE**. And you can put our very best ideas for **TRICKS AND TREATS**— cleverly packaged candies and other Halloween delights—to good use this year and for many haunted holidays to come.

PREVIOUS Carved Pumpkins, see page 183 for basic how-to

PUMPKINS GALORE

CARVED BLACK PUMPKIN

An oversize pumpkin gets a startling makeover with some black floral paint and a glowing cat cutout. Carve the pumpkin following the basic instructions on page 183, using the cat template (see page 358), with one addition: Before transferring the design, wrap masking tape around the stem and coat the hollowed-out pumpkin with black floral spray. Let dry completely before you start carving, then remove tape and continue with your creation. For a muted glow, tack a sheet of waxed paper behind the cutout.

pumpkin-carving techniques

With a handful of versatile tools and a few fundamental techniques, you can create a wide variety of effects. See for yourself in the pumpkin projects that follow.

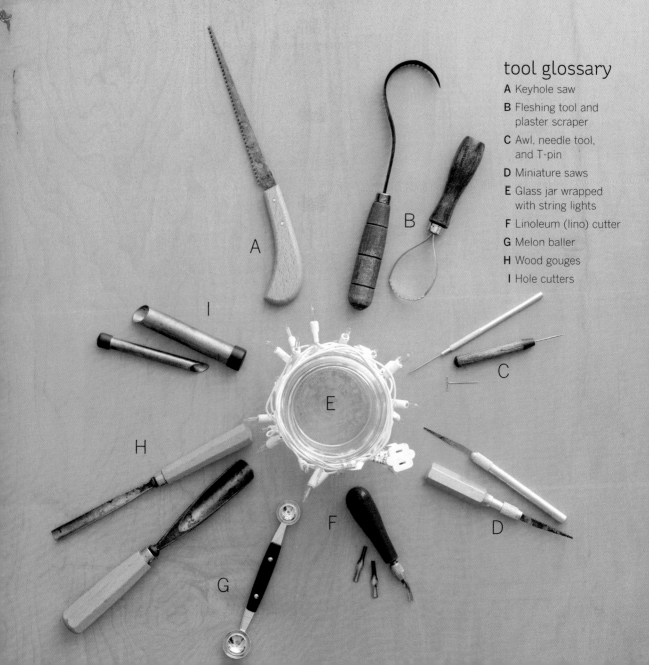

tool glossary

A Keyhole saw

B Fleshing tool and plaster scraper

C Awl, needle tool, and T-pin

D Miniature saws

E Glass jar wrapped with string lights

F Linoleum (lino) cutter

G Melon baller

H Wood gouges

I Hole cutters

the basics

1 CUT A HOLE Whether the design is simple or complicated, all carved pumpkins start out the same way: by cutting the pumpkin open and hollowing it out. Using a keyhole saw (A), cut an opening in the top, bottom, or side of your pumpkin, depending on your intended project.

2 SCOOP OUT THE FLESH Remove the inner flesh with a large metal spoon. Use a plaster scraper or fleshing tool (B) to thin the pumpkin's walls to a thickness of ½ to ¾ inch.

3 MARK YOUR DESIGN When you're ready to carve a design, download and print a template (sized as desired to fit your pumpkin) or draw your own; tape template to pumpkin and use an awl or T-pin (C) to poke holes along the outline of the design. Remove the template.

4 START CARVING Using the holes as a guide, carve out the details of your design with a miniature saw's small, sturdy blade (D). When you're ready to illuminate your carved pumpkin, string lights are preferable to candles for most designs. Wrap a strand of 20 lights around a glass jar (E) and secure wires with tape. Cut a hole in the hollowed-out pumpkin for the cord, and place the jar inside.

special effects

LINOLEUM CUTTER Use this tool (F) and its interchangeable blades to carve a detailed design into the surface of a pumpkin with accuracy.

MELON BALLER Carve spherical chunks out of the shell of a pumpkin with this common kitchen utensil (G).

WOOD GOUGES Create stripes of varying widths in the shell of the pumpkin using one of these carpentry tools (H).

HOLE CUTTERS Short metal pipes (I) with a sharp end and a capped one work best for cutting out perfect circles.

carved pumpkin block-printing

A menacing trio of jack-o'-lanterns makes a thrilling centerpiece on a party table (opposite). All three are carved with graphic Halloween icons—witch, screeching cat, and unfurled bat— then their raised surfaces are painted black. The technique used to create them produces bold, dramatic imagery that's perfect for block-printing onto paper and fabric. We used the bat image to print a whole branchful on a pair of white gauze curtains. Owls, vultures, and wicked witches, all well-known symbols of Halloween, adorn luminaria (above) and help set the mood for an eerie outdoor party. For the pumpkin carving instructions, see page 186; block-printing instructions are on page 187.

carved-pumpkin silhouettes

Silhouettes offer a sophisticated variation on pumpkin carving, whether you block-print with them or not. Carve pumpkins in several different designs, and you'll end up with a haunting houseful of boldly graphic jack-o'-lanterns.

WHAT YOU WILL NEED Carved-pumpkin silhouette templates (optional; see page 358), pumpkins, low-tack masking tape, awl or T-pin, linoleum cutter, wax pencil, wood gouge, petroleum jelly, brayer, lino ink (a water-soluble printing ink) or black acrylic paint, paintbrush, string lights, glass jar

1 Download and print templates (or draw your own design), sizing as desired. Follow the basic instructions on page 183 to cut a hole in the pumpkin and scrape out flesh (thin the wall behind the design to about ½ inch thick so light can shine through). Tape the template onto the pumpkin, and transfer the image by punching holes along the design with an awl or T-pin.

2 Remove template. Using a linoleum cutter with a fine-tip blade, carve outline and interior features of image (do not cut all the way through the flesh).

3 Draw a frame around design with a wax pencil. Using a wood gouge and then a linoleum cutter with a wide-tip blade, carve away rind inside the frame, cutting ¼ inch deep so design is in clear relief. Rub petroleum jelly on exposed flesh to repel ink drips and slow decay (if ink does stray, cut away stain).

4 Coat brayer with lino ink, if using to print (see instructions opposite); otherwise, use acrylic paint. Roll brayer onto design. Fill in any missed areas with a paintbrush. Wrap jar with string lights; place inside pumpkin.

pumpkin block prints

To print designs in relief, carved pumpkins work just as well as more commonly used block printing materials such as linoleum, wood, and potatoes.

WHAT YOU WILL NEED Pumpkins with silhouettes (see instructions, opposite), brayer, lino ink or acrylic paint, Japanese rice paper, paintbrush (optional), muslin or other cloth, curtain rod

FOR PRINTING ON PAPER This technique works on most paper, but Japanese rice paper picks up ink especially well and produces prints that look aged. The illustrations at left show a sheet of paper, but you can easily adapt the technique to print on paper bags, as for the luminaria (see page 185). Press a piece of paper against the inked image on the pumpkin, using your fingers to make sure paper touches all inked areas. (Rice paper is very thin, so you will see the image form as you work.) Peel away paper gently; let dry. Touch up print with paint and paintbrush, if necessary. For more prints, repeat, reinking each time.

FOR PRINTING ON FABRIC Pumpkin-printing on fabric is as straightforward as on paper, but because fabric is limper, it requires more careful handling. The bat image works nicely with this technique—when you line up the prints, the animals all appear to be hanging from one branch. Begin by laying the top of the cloth (we used muslin) against a carved and inked pumpkin; rub until the design appears on the cloth. Carefully remove cloth. Wait a few minutes to let the ink set; then repeat across the width of the cloth. Let dry. To make a curtain panel, fold the top edge over, and sew a channel to fit the curtain rod. Hang the curtain so that the printed side faces the room.

carved-pumpkin village

A group of historic-looking pumpkin "houses," complete with architectural details, is arranged within a twig fence to create a haunted hamlet for Halloween. All of the houses have roofs, so the pumpkins are cut from the bottom. The ground floor of each two-story house also gets a hole in the top, so light can travel all the way up. Use a miniature saw or sharp knife to cut holes, then scrape out the flesh to a thickness of about ½ inch (see page 183 for basic instructions).

WHAT YOU WILL NEED Pumpkins, grease pencil, pumpkin village templates (optional; see page 358), miniature saw or sharp knife, ridged square cookie cutter, linoleum cutter, straight pins, wood gouge, rubbing alcohol, string lights, glass jar, twigs and leaves, hot-glue gun

1 With a grease pencil, draw doors and windows on pumpkins (or use the pumpkin village templates); cut out with the miniature saw or a sharp knife. For shutters with wavy edges (which suggest louvers), press the ridged cookie cutter into a piece cut from the window, then cut that piece in half. Extend "louvers" on each shutter by scoring horizontal lines across it with a linoleum cutter. To hang doors and shutters, push heads of straight pins into cut edges, and attach to pumpkin.

2 To simulate shingles, press wood gouge shallowly into pumpkin top, making rows all the way around the stem. Remove any remaining grease pencil marks with rubbing alcohol.

3 Wrap jar with string lights; place inside pumpkin. Arrange pumpkins among twigs and leaves, and surround village with a fence made of twigs, hot-glued together.

carved-pumpkin owls

A band of inquisitive owls keeps lookout along a porch wall. Their bulging eyes are made from mini pumpkins and gourds, and glow from within thanks to bundles of string lights. Curved pieces of pumpkin stand in for feet and ears. These instructions can be adapted to create the facial details of other pumpkin animals; let the shapes of your pumpkins inspire the species you choose.

WHAT YOU WILL NEED Pumpkins (one for each body, plus small ones to cut into pieces for ears, nose, and feet), pen, mini pumpkins or gourds (for the eyes), drill (with a ⅝-inch bit) or large hole cutter, string lights, rubber bands, toothpicks, glass jar, electrical tape, wood gouge or linoleum cutter, miniature saw

1 Follow instructions on page 183 to cut a hole in the large pumpkin and scoop out the insides. Make eye holes: Mark with a pen, then drill or cut with the hole cutter. In the tops of 2 mini pumpkins, cut holes slightly larger than eye holes; scoop out insides. Drill a small hole in the bottom of each mini pumpkin. From inside larger pumpkin, push four lights through each eye hole, securing the bottom of the bundle with a rubber band to keep the bulbs from touching one another. Use toothpicks to attach mini pumpkins over lights. Wrap more lights around a glass jar, securing wires with tape, and place inside large pumpkin.

2 To add "feather" details, use a wood gouge or linoleum cutter to make graduated rows of half circles in the pumpkin skin.

3 Cut ear, nose, and feet shapes from small pumpkins with a miniature saw; attach in place with toothpicks.

leaf-carved lanterns

Trick-or-treaters and guests will feel more welcome than wary ascending a staircase lit up with leaf-carved pumpkin lanterns. The botanical motifs are produced using a variety of basic carving techniques. The resulting patterns are as varied as fallen leaves, which provide the only templates you'll need.

WHAT YOU WILL NEED Pumpkins, fallen leaves, tape, grease pencil, linoleum cutter (with a narrow blade), long miniature saw, glass jar, string lights

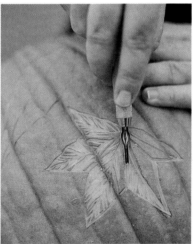

1 Cut a hole in the pumpkin's top or bottom, and scoop out the insides (see page 183 for basic instructions). Tape leaves to pumpkin and trace around each with a grease pencil; remove leaves.

2 Instead of cutting out the entire leaf shape, use a linoleum cutter with a narrow blade to peel away the rind and expose the flesh, producing decorative motifs of your choice or realistic-looking "veins."

3 Alternatively, cut out the entire leaf shape. Using a long miniature saw, cut out part of the leaf to make thin details, such as veins. Reposition the embellished leaf, letting it protrude slightly. To light the pumpkins, place a glass jar wrapped with string lights in the cavity.

silly pumpkin faces

A whole host of deranged-looking characters have taken up residence in a bookshelf, among a collection of black basalt Wedgwood stoneware. But never fear: These grinning creatures aren't dangerous, they're just a little crazy. Their expressions are modeled after cardboard jack-o'-lanterns from the early twentieth century. Create your own funny faces by carving basic shapes into hollowed-out pumpkins and pinning the clip-art paper features to the inside.

WHAT YOU WILL NEED Pumpkins, silly pumpkin face clip art (see page 358), heavyweight paper, grease pencil, scissors, miniature saw, map tack pins

1 Cut a hole in the bottom of a pumpkin and scoop out the insides (see page 183 for basic instructions). Download and print the clip art to desired size onto heavyweight paper; cut out. Lay out your design. Using a grease pencil, draw eye, nose, and mouth shapes that are slightly smaller than the paper facial features and cut out with the miniature saw.

2 Using map tack pins, attach features behind their corresponding cutouts. There is no need to illuminate these decorations.

papier-mâché pumpkins

The stairway in an entry hall serves as the perfect landing spot for a set of handmade paper jack-o'-lanterns in graduated sizes. For safety, these beaming faces are lit from within by battery-powered lights. A single sheet of tissue pasted inside diffuses the light and hides the working parts; floral wire and tape make optional stem and tendrils.

WHAT YOU WILL NEED Balloons, glass jars, wheat paste, tissue paper (in orange and yellow), paintbrush, clothespins and clothesline, small scissors, craft knife, floral wire, cotton balls, floral tape, pencil

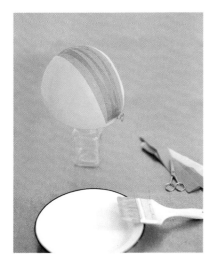

1 Begin by blowing up a balloon and tying it off. Rest balloon on an empty jar. Dab wheat paste on a small section of the balloon and drape a strip of orange tissue paper vertically from the balloon's crown to its knot. Using the paintbrush, apply wheat paste evenly over the strip. Add another strip so that it slightly overlaps the first, and brush on more paste. Continue around the balloon until it is covered completely. After two layers of orange tissue, apply two layers of yellow.

2 Using clothespins, hang covered balloons on the clothesline by their knots. When they are completely dry, pop each balloon by snipping with scissors as you hold the knot. Remove the balloon through the hole around the knot.

3 To cut a lid, make an incision in the knot end with a craft knife. Finish cutting out with scissors. Remove a small circle from the other end to create a base. Mark and cut out eyes, nose, and mouth. On the inside, cover these holes with a single layer of tissue paper (apply paste to edges of tissue before positioning). For the stem, push 3 different lengths of floral wire through the knot hole in the lid. (Stuff a cotton ball in the underside of the hole; secure with floral tape.) Wrap each piece of wire in floral tape, and then wrap all 3 pieces together to create the base of the stem. Wrap the free ends of the wires around a pencil to resemble tendrils.

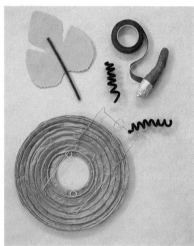

patch-o'-lanterns

Take an ordinary paper lantern, dress it up with leaves, a stem, and tendrils,
and it will assume a totally unexpected identity—that of a pumpkin. A few craft
supplies are all you need to transform the inexpensive globes.

WHAT YOU WILL NEED Leaf template (see page 358), scissors, pencil, green paper, white craft glue, pipe cleaners (in dark green and brown), marker, paper lantern, newspaper, brown floral tape, monofilament

Download and print the leaf template to desired size; cut out. Trace onto green paper and cut out. Glue a dark green pipe cleaner to the leaf's center. For the tendrils, spiral two brown pipe cleaners around a marker, then slide off. Attach leaf and tendrils to a lantern by winding the ends of pipe cleaners around the lantern's wire frame. For the stem, roll a few sheets of newspaper into a tapered shape; cut off the wider end. Starting at the thinner end, wrap with brown floral tape. To attach stem to lantern, continue to wrap brown floral tape around stem and wire frame. Hang the lanterns with monofilament.

glittered pumpkins

Pumpkins that sparkle and shine add a touch of glamour to tables and serving areas, and they should last longer than jack-o'-lanterns.

WHAT YOU WILL NEED Paintbrush, white craft glue, small pumpkins, paper plate or newspaper, powder glitter (in combinations of pink, red, and champagne), brown acrylic paint

With a paintbrush, spread glue over the surface of a small pumpkin. Working over a paper plate or newspaper to catch excess, sprinkle powder glitter over pumpkin, covering completely. Let dry for about one hour, then shake off the excess over the paper plate. Coat stem with brown acrylic paint; let dry.

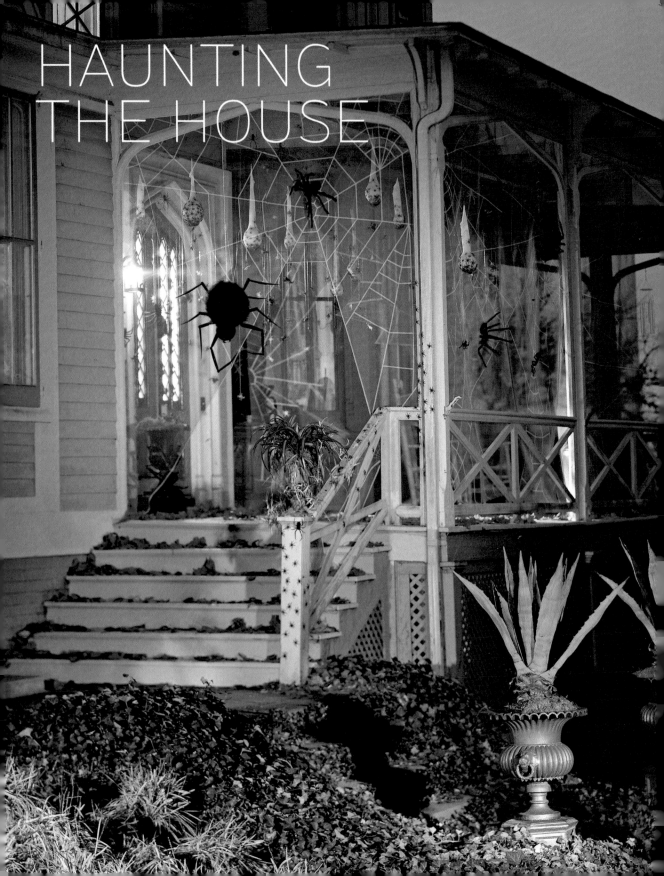

HAUNTING
THE HOUSE

infested entrance

Arachnophobes, beware: This terrifyingly larger-than-life spiderweb bars entry to the house; an opening in the web is the only way to pass through.

WHAT YOU WILL NEED Fiberglass window screening (100-foot roll), scissors, kraft paper or newspaper, chalk, yardstick, white paint marker (available online), pushpins or removable adhesive hooks, paintbrush, large paper or plastic spider (available at party-supply stores), black acrylic paint, 2 Styrofoam balls (1 large and 1 small), serrated knife, hot-glue gun, black faux fur (optional), 2 red beads, straight pins, monofilament

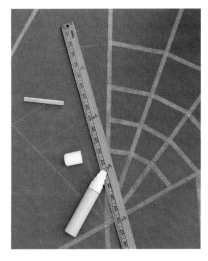 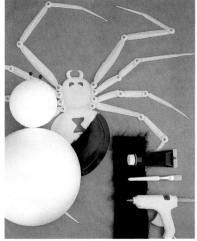

FOR WEBBED ENTRY Cut the fiberglass window screening to desired size (based on entryway). Lay screening on kraft paper or newspaper to protect your work surface. Mark the web's center with chalk, and draw radiating lines using a yardstick as a guide. Connect the lines to make a web pattern; add smaller webs in the corners. Using the paint marker and yardstick, color over chalk lines. Once paint is dry, cut out a triangular entrance, using web lines as a guide. Snip edges randomly for a jagged look. Tack screen to porch using pushpins or adhesive hooks.

FOR SPIDER Using a paintbrush, coat the spider with black paint. Cut the foam balls in half with a serrated knife: You'll need one foam ball that's slightly larger than the spider's head, and one slightly larger than its body. Paint one large half and one small half black (save the others for another use); let dry. Use hot glue to cover larger foam ball with strips of black faux fur, if desired. Hot-glue the halved balls to the head and body. For each eye, slide a red bead onto a straight pin and press it into the top of the foam head. To hang the spider in front of its web, pin a length of monofilament to the body, and attach the other end to the ceiling with a pushpin or removable adhesive hooks.

dastardly table decorations and paper spiderwebs

Holiday party decor needn't be costly or fussy. Here, inexpensive fabric and black crepe paper transform a sumptuous cookies-and-coffee buffet into a sinister spread. We covered the table in gauze and then affixed black tissue-paper tatters to the perimeter of the table and to a pair of cake stands piled high with sweets. Card-stock spiderwebs hang from above— spun, perhaps, by the store-bought arachnid dangling nearby.

WHAT YOU WILL NEED Black tissue paper, ruler, scissors, straightedge, rotary cutter (fitted with a decorative wave blade), cutting mat, double-sided tape, spiderweb template (see page 358), card stock (in white and black), white pencil, craft knife, monofilament

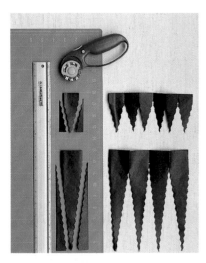

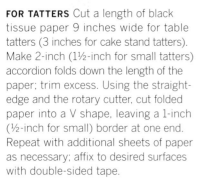

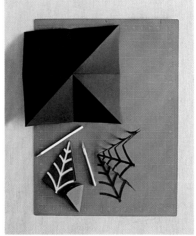

FOR TATTERS Cut a length of black tissue paper 9 inches wide for table tatters (3 inches for cake stand tatters). Make 2-inch (1½-inch for small tatters) accordion folds down the length of the paper; trim excess. Using the straight-edge and the rotary cutter, cut folded paper into a V shape, leaving a 1-inch (½-inch for small) border at one end. Repeat with additional sheets of paper as necessary; affix to desired surfaces with double-sided tape.

FOR SPIDERWEBS Download and print small and large spiderweb templates onto white card stock; cut out. Fold a square sheet of black card stock (12-inch for a small web, or 18-inch for a large web) in half diagonally, then fold in half twice more to form a small triangle. Trace template onto folded card stock with a white pencil; use a craft knife to cut out pattern. Unfold and hang with monofilament.

bird silhouette windows

This once-normal home is suddenly overrun with a flock of enormous reveling raptors. The birds are cut from black plastic weed barrier, available at garden centers. They can be hung with curtain rods or simply tacked to window frames, and are easily stored for use year after year.

WHAT YOU WILL NEED Bird silhouette templates (see page 358), scissors, chalk, yardstick, black plastic weed barrier, semi-sheer white fabric, measuring tape, needle and thread (or sewing machine), fabric glue, curtain rods and mounting hardware (optional), pushpins or removable adhesive hooks

1 Download and print tiled full-size templates. Tape together and cut out. Trace onto a black plastic weed barrier using chalk. Cut out. (Alternatively, use the grid method to transfer the templates onto the barrier. Print the grid method template so you can see the details of the pattern. Determine how wide you want the image in inches; divide that width by the number of squares in the template's width. That number is the size you should make each square in the grid. Use chalk and a yardstick to create the grid on the barrier. Trace the bird freehand with chalk, copying the image square by square. Cut out.)

2 Cut a piece of semi-sheer white fabric a few inches longer and wider than your window frame (if hanging from a curtain rod, add 4 inches to the length to accommodate a channel). Hem fabric; sew channel for curtain rod, if using.

3 Apply fabric glue all the way around the edges of the bird silhouette and on center of fabric; adhere bird to fabric.

4 Let dry completely before hanging in window with curtain rod, if using; otherwise, use pushpins or removable adhesive hooks.

glittered skeleton parts

A tall glass dome displays a collection of frightening—yet faux—remains. Artificial skulls and bones, available from online educational-supply companies, are coated in shades of shimmering green and silver glitter, then stacked for eerie effect.

WHAT YOU WILL NEED Newspaper or kraft paper, artificial skulls and bones, hot-glue gun (optional), paintbrush, tacky glue, large shallow bowl, ultrafine opaque glitter (in green and silver), plastic spoon, plate or tray for drying

Cover work surface with paper. Before applying the glitter, remove any springs and screws from skulls and bones; if the pieces require assembly, secure with a glue gun. Using a paintbrush, apply tacky glue to half of a skull or bone. Hold object over a bowl filled with glitter. Spoon glitter over glued surface, making certain the glitter falls into all the crevices and sockets and any excess lands back in the bowl. Place on a plate or tray. Let dry for at least 1 hour. Tap or brush off any excess glitter. Repeat gluing and glittering uncoated surfaces of each piece until completely covered, and touch up other areas as needed.

GLITTERED BONE PLACE SETTING
Glittered plastic skeletal hands create a suitably dramatic—and unexpectedly artful—ambience when set off by a lusterware plate. Follow the same glittering instructions as for the skulls (see opposite). Let dry. Write each guest's name on a place card; carefully set between the glittered bony fingers.

jar-o'-lanterns

A bit of paint and a stencil cut from masking tape help ordinary glass jars come to life as custom candy containers.

WHAT YOU WILL NEED Clean glass jar, paintbrush, oil-based enamel paints (orange, yellow, and black), extra-wide masking tape, jar-o'-lantern template (optional; see page 358), marker, craft knife, plastic-covered 20-gauge wire, needle-nose pliers, wire cutters

1 Working in a well-ventilated area, coat the inside of a jar with orange or yellow paint. Apply a square of masking tape to the outside of each jar. Press out any air bubbles. Use a marker to draw face on tape. Cut out features with a craft knife to form a stencil. (Alternatively, download and print jar-o'-lantern templates, cut out features, and secure over the tape; cut around them to form stencil.)

2 Using black paint and a brush, fill in the features of the stencil. Let paint dry completely, then carefully peel off and discard tape.

3 For a handle, loop one end of the wire with pliers. Make a lasso shape to hug the neck of the jar. Bend remaining wire over for a handle. Cut wire; make another loop to hook onto ring. Slip ring over jar's mouth; tighten as necessary.

vampire bat piñata

A swooping papier-mâché bat is sure to be a scream at any Halloween fête. You might want to wear gloves when making the piñata, since black tissue will stain your hands when damp. Before you start, tear some newspaper into strips; use the rest to cover your work surface.

WHAT YOU WILL NEED Two balloons (one large for the body and one small for the head), 2 empty jars or bowls, white craft glue, medium artist's paintbrush, newspaper, black tissue paper (cut into strips), latex gloves (optional), string, clothespins and clothesline, craft knife, candy, confetti, bat piñata templates (see page 358), white card stock, small scissors, white pencil, black poster board, black duct tape, tacks

1 Blow up and tie off balloons, and rest them on empty jars. Brush diluted craft glue—2 parts glue to 1 part water—on a small section of a balloon, from crown to knot, then drape a strip of paper over glue (start with newspaper). Brush the strip with more glue. Repeat, slightly overlapping strips, until each balloon is covered (with knot exposed) with four layers of newspaper, then with black tissue. (When making bat body from large balloon, stop after two layers of newspaper and tie a long piece of string around center, for hanging; continue layering with paper.) With clothespins, hang balloons on clothesline and let dry overnight.

2 Cut a hole in the top of the body with the craft knife (save the piece to make the ears); remove balloon (it will pop when you cut the hole). Fill the body with candy and confetti. Cover the cut edge with tissue paper. Pop and remove the balloon from the smaller piece. Place the bat head onto the body. Use several layers of tissue paper to secure the head to the body, brushing with diluted glue. Let dry. Download and print the face templates on white card stock (or draw features by hand). Cut out features; attach with undiluted glue. Cut ears from reserved piece; glue in place.

3 Sketch large wing shapes on black poster board; cut out. Secure wings to the sides of the bat's body with the duct tape. Glue black tissue paper over the taped joints. Next, tape a length of string to the end of each wing; cover tape with tissue paper. Hang bat from body string. Tack the wing strings to the ceiling so bat looks as if it is flying.

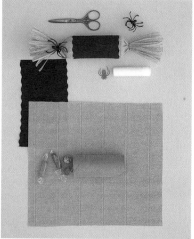

creepy candy "crackers"

Brightly colored treat holders—modeled after British Christmas crackers—beg to be ripped open by happy little Halloween revelers. Don't expect a loud bang, though: While store-bought crackers have a noisemaker inside, these do not (a boon for grown-ups and ghouls who prefer a little peace and quiet).

WHAT YOU WILL NEED Scissors and/or scalloping shears, crepe paper (orange, black, or white), colored paper (orange or black), stickers or letter stamps and ink pads, cardboard paper tubes, candy or other tiny treats, glue stick, twine, plastic spider or bat rings

For each package, cut an 11-inch square of crepe paper and a 4-by-7-inch rectangle of paper in another color (use scalloping shears for decorative edges, if desired). Decorate colored paper with stickers or stamps. Fill a paper tube with candy or other treats, and roll crepe paper around tube; glue seams closed. Wrap paper rectangle around center; glue. Tie ends with twine to secure, and snip ends to form fringe, if desired. Slip plastic rings over twine. To open, pull from both ends (or share with a friend, each pulling one end).

pumpkin pouch party favors

Little witches and ghosts will find it hard to resist tearing into crinkly crepe-paper pumpkins filled with an assortment of holiday surprises. We stuffed the pouches with candies and tiny plastic toys.

WHAT YOU WILL NEED Orange crepe paper, scissors, ruler, candy and plastic toys, green floral tape, pencil

For each pouch, cut two 10-inch-diameter circles from crepe paper. Stack two circles and pile goodies such as candy or plastic toys in the center. Gather the outer edges of the paper around the treats to form a pouch. Grasp the paper just above the treats, and twist a little. Secure by wrapping floral tape around the base of the twist, binding upward to create a pumpkin "stem." If necessary, trim excess paper before binding. Tendrils can be made by wrapping a length of floral tape around a pencil; tie tendrils around stems.

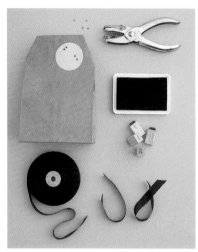

full-moon favor bags

Plain brown-paper lunch bags turn trick-or-treat-worthy when embellished with yellow moons and tiny bats.

WHAT YOU WILL NEED Brown paper lunch bags, alphabet and punctuation stamps, black ink pad, candy, yellow paper, circle craft punch or scissors, glue stick, hole punch, black seam binding, pinking shears

Stamp bags with "Trick?" or "Treat?" and then fill with candy. Fold corners back. Fold top of bag down 1½ inches. Make a 2-inch yellow paper moon using circle punch or by tracing a round object and cutting out. Glue moon to front of bag in top right corner. Punch two small holes through moon and bag, ¼ inch apart. Repeat in another spot on moon. Cut two 5-inch pieces of seam binding and thread through holes; knot to form bats (they will also secure bag). Trim bat wings diagonally with pinking shears.

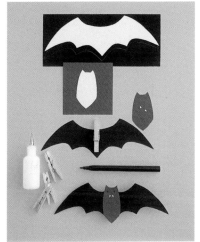

batty bag clips

A flurry of night flyers is delighted to hold candy for otherwise occupied little hands. Attached to clothespins, the bats can be clipped to cellophane bags or to the rims of serving bowls on a buffet table.

WHAT YOU WILL NEED Batty bag clip templates (see page 358), scissors, construction paper (black and brown), white craft glue, clothespins, black marker, white paper, cellophane bags, candy

Download and print templates and cut out. Trace the wing template onto black construction paper and the body template onto brown; cut out both shapes. Affix wings to a clothespin using glue. Draw eyes on body with black marker and glue two tiny white paper triangles just beneath them for fangs. Glue the bat's body onto the wings. Let dry completely before clipping.

illuminated trick-or-treat bag
Light up the night with trick-or-treat bags adorned with bright-eyed bats.

WHAT YOU WILL NEED Paper plate, reflective paint, paintbrush, illuminated trick-or-treat bag template (see page 358), card stock, black paper, scissors, ⅛-inch hole punch or nail, white craft glue, battery-operated LED lights, black paper shopping bag

Coat the bottom of a paper plate with bold reflective paint. Download and print the template onto card stock. Cut out. Trace onto black paper. Cut out. Create eyes with a hole punch or nail, first in bats, then in plate. Affix bats to plate with glue (the eye holes should fit directly over the holes in the paper plate). Stick bulbs from battery-operated LED lights through each eye. Near the bottom of the black paper bag, cut a hole for the battery pack to slide through. Place battery pack in bag. Attach plate to bag over hole with glue.

self-serve halloween party favors

Set out an oversized pumpkin covered with goody bags that kids can grab themselves—either at a party or on the porch. Decorate small plain flat paper bags with rubber-stamped designs, fill with treats, and attach to pumpkin with thumbtacks. Then attach a note on a mini chalkboard inviting kids to help themselves.

TABLETOP ACCENTS

CORNHUSK-FLOWER NAPKIN RINGS Delicate, rosy-hued apple blossoms, crafted from crepe-paper-like dried cornhusks, crown a set of rustic napkin rings. See page 223 for instructions.

oak leaf napkin rings and mini cornucopia

Small glints and gleams can make a great impression on the Thanksgiving table. A cleverly folded napkin and a handwoven sparkling cornucopia favor (see photograph on page 218) echo the horn of plenty's shape; more gilded leaves and acorns festoon the napkin ring and the place card.

WHAT YOU WILL NEED Acorns, T-pin, 6-inch lengths of 26-gauge gold or copper wire, paintbrush, water-based size adhesive (available at crafts stores), cotton gloves, faux gold leaf, small soft-bristle brush, hot-glue gun, brown floral tape, oak leaves, napkins, ½-inch-wide gold ribbon, gold lametta (¼-inch tinsel roping; you will need 10 feet for each cornucopia), scissors, Styrofoam cone

FOR THE NAPKIN RINGS Remove caps from acorns; set nuts aside. Poke 2 holes in the top of each cap with the T-pin. Thread fine wire through holes, and twist ends together. Repeat with remaining caps; set aside. Paint nuts with water-based size adhesive. Let dry. In a draft-free room, wear gloves to lift 1 gold-leaf sheet from packet. Tear off a piece, and wrap it around the nut. Smooth it with your fingers. Use the small brush to even out the texture of the gold leaf and remove any flakes. Repeat process to gild remaining nuts. Hot-glue nuts to their caps. Let dry. Wrap each acorn wire

"stem" tightly with brown floral tape. Gild 1 side of each oak leaf in gold leaf, following the same procedure as for the acorn. With the hot-glue gun, secure wire to the back of each oak leaf. Let dry. Make a cluster of leaves and acorns by wrapping their wires together with brown floral tape; do not snip wire. Repeat. Roll a napkin into a cone shape, and tie with the gold ribbon. Slip an oak-leaf cluster into the ribbon knot. Curl ribbon ends.

FOR THE MINI CORNUCOPIA Cut four 7-inch pieces and one 4-inch piece of lametta. Twist the long pieces together at their midpoints to

create a star with 8 points. Hook the end of the short piece to the center to add a ninth point. Trim ends to same length; space evenly. Hook end of a 7½-foot length of lametta near center of star. Trim Styrofoam cone so it measures 4 inches long. Place tip at center of star; secure with the T-pin. Press the 9 lametta lengths against the cone. Tightly weave remaining lametta through the lengths until all but ¼ inch of the cone is covered. Remove cone. Bend ends over last row. Curve the tip of the cornucopia.

cornhusk-flower napkin rings

Dried cornhusk "petals" can be cut to form nearly any simple flower shape. Husks are naturally off-white or purple; soak the two together to produce a pink hue. For the napkin rings (see photograph on page 221), three shades of cornhusk apple blossoms were attached to wire with floral tape. Although the tiny blooms look intricate, they are easy to produce in quantity. Together, they offer a celebration of the fruits of the harvest while evoking the promise of a vibrant growing season to come.

WHAT YOU WILL NEED Dried cornhusks (available at specialty grocers), paper towels, cornhusk-flower napkin ring templates (see page 358), card stock, scissors, 32-gauge wire, brown floral tape

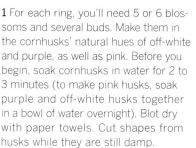

1 For each ring, you'll need 5 or 6 blossoms and several buds. Make them in the cornhusks' natural hues of off-white and purple, as well as pink. Before you begin, soak cornhusks in water for 2 to 3 minutes (to make pink husks, soak purple and off-white husks together in a bowl of water overnight). Blot dry with paper towels. Cut shapes from husks while they are still damp.

2 Download and print templates onto card stock; cut out. Cut out the blossom center, and fold on the dotted line (on blossom center template). Roll tightly to form a stamen; wrap twice with a 3-foot length of the wire. Accordion-fold a cornhusk. Place a petal template on the folded husk, and cut out the shape (producing several petals). Attach five petals around the stamen, wrapping each twice with wire. Cut out the rectangle for a bud, and roll it lengthwise. Wrap with another length of wire, two-thirds down the roll. Open the top of the husk, fold it down halfway, and wrap on itself; wire again.

3 To form the rings, wrap floral tape from the base of each blossom and bud, 2 inches down the stem. Cluster the blossoms and buds, one at a time, securing the wires together with floral tape. Trim the ends to form a 2-inch-diameter ring. Secure the end into the top of the cluster to close the loop.

napkin-folding techniques

A holiday meal deserves an equally festive table. It's easy to add a bit of flourish to each setting with an artfully folded napkin. If you are expecting a sizable crowd for dinner, start folding early. The four classic designs shown here work with square napkins, preferably linen or cotton. Be sure to starch them, and press each fold as you work. The result will be one snappy-looking set of napkins.

ENVELOPE FOLD These simple steps are among the easiest to follow. Once folded, the napkins stack well, and are appropriate for a formal meal as well as a more casual one. This works with any size square napkin (though etiquette experts agree a dinner napkin should be at least 20 inches square).

1 Fold napkin in half diagonally, letting the bottom edge show about ⅛ inch; press the fold.

2 Fold in the 2 bottom corners of the triangle so they meet at the center.

3 Then fold the sides over so they meet at the center.

4 Fold up the bottom half of the napkin to about ½ inch below the triangle flap.

5 Fold the top flap down, closing envelope, and press to finish.

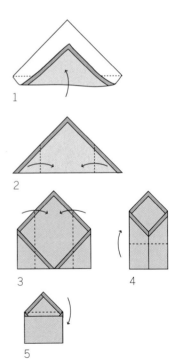

MODERN FOLD Give your guests something pleasant to behold—and to unroll—with this striking contemporary design.

1 Crease a napkin into thirds.

2 Fold along the creases.

3 From the center point, crease the napkin down on the left side at a 45-degree angle; repeat on the right.

4 The napkin now has a tentlike shape.

5 Flip the napkin over; roll up both overhangs.

6 Holding the napkin, including the rolls, flip it.

7 Fold the right and left corners up at 45-degree angles, and place at each table setting.

MENU FOLD Perfect for slipping a menu between the creases, this fold looks particularly pretty with hemstitch-bordered napkins.

1 Fold a napkin in half toward you to form a rectangle. (If the napkin has a wrong side, begin with that side up.)

2 Fold the top layer of the napkin back (away from you), making a new fold one-third of the way in from the open edge.

3 Fold the bottom layer of the napkin in the same direction, so that it partially overlaps the top layer, creating 3 equal-size bands.

4 Fold the napkin crosswise into equal thirds, and press.

5 Fold the left-hand third back and in half so it meets the outside edge; fold the middle third back to meet the opposite outside edge.

LOTUS FOLD Also called the water lily or artichoke, this fold will be familiar to anyone who ever made a paper fortune teller as a child. The center provides the perfect spot to place a dinner roll, party favor, or place card.

1 Fold a napkin in half diagonally both ways; press to crease. Unfold the napkin, flip it over, and fold the top corners to the center point.

2 Repeat with the bottom corners, so all four meet at the center.

3 Flip the napkin over, and fold the corners in to meet at the center.

4 With a finger pressing down on the center of the napkin, reach underneath and pull up the flap at each corner to create the lotus-like petals.

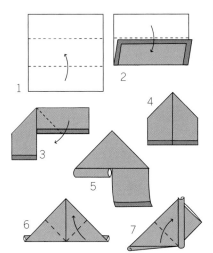

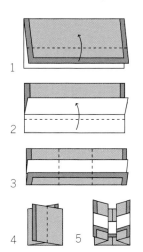

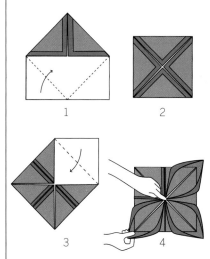

four easy place card ideas

Nothing makes guests feel so welcome as finding their own name at a seat around the table. Here are several lovely—and fast—ways to mark their spots.

modern fold napkin with autumn leaf

A leaf in the folds of a napkin and a handwritten place card—a strip of paper inscribed with a white gel-ink pen—beckon each guest to dinner. Follow the directions for the Modern Fold napkin on page 225. Place a napkin, point forward, on a plate. Nestle a clean maple leaf in the fold and place a handwritten strip of paper in front of the leaf.

pomegranate and "leaf"

Rosy pomegranates anchor simple name tags while adding a splash of color to a neutral place setting. Use scissors or pinking shears to cut a simple leaf shape from card stock or art paper. Write a guest's name on the leaf, punch a hole at one end, and attach to a pomegranate with a toothpick.

gilded gourds

Pumpkins aren't just for Halloween. These autumnal main-stays might seem a bit humble for a formal Thanksgiving meal, but dress them in gold and they'll fit right in. Here, a miniature pumpkin painted with gold floral spray brightens a table set with linens in shades of blue. The pumpkins can also serve as take-home favors. After letting the painted pumpkins dry, simply tie a card to each stem using thin gold cord, and write each guest's name in gold ink.

walnut shells

Nuts are always abundant at holiday time, and here they are put to use as adorable place card holders. To create walnut name labels, cut slips of paper into flags (about 1½ inches by ½ inch each). Write names on the paper using a fine-tipped felt or metallic-paint pen. Open shells slightly with a nutcracker, if needed, and insert a flag into each.

glittered table decorations

Though it sparkles and shines, there's an elegant simplicity in this Thanksgiving table setting. A few organic elements, enlivened with a bit of gilding, evoke fall's abundance. Stripes of glitter adorn the edge of a table runner; to make the eye-catching centerpiece, we filled a large glass compote with glittered Indian corn and squash.

WHAT YOU WILL NEED Masking tape, fabric table runner, washable fabric glue, foam brush, fine glitter (in gold, sapphire, and gray), kraft paper, dried corn, white craft glue, gourds

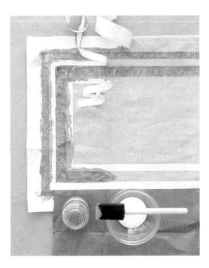 

FOR THE GLITTERED TABLE RUNNER
Alternate strips of masking tape with fabric along the table runner's border, as shown. Press tape firmly against fabric so glue won't seep. Working in 10-inch sections, apply fabric glue to outer stripe with a foam brush, then sprinkle with glitter. Let dry for at least 4 hours, then shake off excess glitter. Cover that stripe with paper, and repeat process for next stripe. We used Florentine Gold on the outer stripe, and mixed Sapphire Blue and Smoky Gray for the inner stripe.

FOR THE GLITTERED CENTERPIECE
Work over paper so you can funnel and reuse extra glitter. Pick some ears of dried corn to glitter fully and other ears to do more sparingly, so your arrangement doesn't go overboard. For the former, coat fully with craft glue and glitter. For the latter, use a foam brush to lightly dab some kernels with craft glue, then apply glitter. To soften husks so you can shape the ears when you arrange them, steam over a kettle of boiling water once the glitter has set. To fill out the arrangements, glitter the stems of a few gourds, and place them among the glittered corn.

four autumnal napkin rings

Along with place cards and other table decorating details, napkin rings offer a chance to make a lovely first impression on your guests. Here are several of our favorite ideas for memorable ones, inspired by the season.

clip-art leaves

These luminous napkin holders look as though they've fallen from an imaginary tree. Download and print the leaf clip art onto card stock (see page 358; you'll get two rings per 8½-by-11-inch sheet). Cut out with a craft knife or scissors. Make two cuts where indicated on each template. Bring ends together, and slide slits into each other to form a ring. Roll up a fabric napkin, and slide inside holder.

acorns and ribbon

Squirrels aren't the only ones who can tap an oak tree's potential. For pretty napkin ties, attach fallen or store-bought acorns to the ends of a length of satin ribbon. Separate the cap from the body of each with a craft knife. Next, make a small hole in the cap with a T-pin. Knot one end of a 9-inch length of ¼-inch brown satin ribbon. Thread the other end through the cap; knot at the top. Thread the ribbon through another cap; knot on both sides. Reattach the acorn bodies with hot glue. Tie ribbon around a folded napkin, letting acorns rest in the center.

star-anise ties

These pretty little fasteners are both functional and fragrant: Delicate star-anise pods secured to lengths of suede cord keep rolled napkins in place while releasing a subtle bouquet into the air. Begin by threading a piece of suede cord (or decorative ribbon) under the stiff stem of the dried spice. (If there is no stem, place a small dab of hot glue on the back of the spice and press it onto the cord; let dry completely before proceeding.) Roll napkins, positioning so the star anise is centered in the front, and tie the cord in the back to secure.

feather wraps

A single feather dresses up a simple twill-tape wrap, and doubles as a headdress during—or better yet, after—the feast for your youngest guests. Cut a piece of twill tape long enough to tie around a child's head, then cut a small hole in the center. Insert a clean feather in the hole, and stitch it to secure it in place. Tie the tape loosely around a folded dinner napkin.

EYE-CATCHING CENTERPIECES

oak leaf cornucopia

The cornucopia, that traditional symbol of autumn's abundance, assumes a stately presence for the harvest feast when coated in shimmering gold and wreathed in gilded oak leaves and acorns. For added glow, burnish the stems of pale gourds spilling from the basket as well. The gilding instructions here call for faux gold leaf (one large sheet covers about six leaves and eight acorns). If you prefer, you can substitute metallic floral spray to good effect (omit the size, gloves, gold leaf, and bristle brush from the list of materials needed).

WHAT YOU WILL NEED Newspaper or kraft paper, 18-inch cornucopia basket, white spray primer, floral spray (in brilliant gold), acorns, T-pin, 26-gauge gold or copper wire, paintbrush, water-based size adhesive (available at crafts stores), cotton gloves, faux gold leaf, soft-bristle brush, hot-glue gun, brown floral tape, oak leaves, gourds

1 Cover your work surface with paper and be sure the area is well ventilated. Spray the basket with primer; let dry. Follow with 1 or 2 coats of floral spray until basket is completely covered; let dry.

2 Remove the cap from each acorn; set the nuts aside. Poke 2 holes in the top of each cap with a T-pin. Thread a 6-inch length of wire through the holes in one cap, and twist the ends together. Repeat with the remaining caps.

3 Paint the nuts with water-based size. Let dry. Working in a draft-free room and wearing gloves, lift 1 gold-leaf sheet from its packet (a large sheet will cover about 8 acorns and 6 leaves). Tear off a piece, and wrap it around a nut. Smooth it with your fingers. Use a soft-bristle brush to even out the texture of the leaf and remove any flakes. Repeat with the remaining nuts. (See first how-to photograph on page 222 for visual reference.)

4 With the hot-glue gun, secure the nuts to their caps. Let dry. Wrap each wire "stem" tightly with brown floral tape.

5 Cover one side of each oak leaf in gold leaf, following step 3. With the hot-glue gun, secure a 6-inch length of wire to the back of each oak leaf. Let dry.

6 Make a cluster of leaves and acorns by wrapping their wires together with floral tape; do not snip the wire. Repeat. Attach each cluster to the next with floral tape until the garland is long enough to cover the basket's rim. Secure with hot glue. Let dry. If desired, gild the gourd stems following the instructions in step 3.

harvest sheaf centerpiece

Wheat symbolizes a fruitful life—making it an appropriate Thanksgiving decoration. Here, one hundred stalks are gathered into a gorgeous display. The final flourish? A luxurious satin ribbon. This arrangement can be made weeks in advance, leaving you time to focus on other details on the big day.

WHAT YOU WILL NEED 100 stalks of wheat (about 6 bunches, available from florists and crafts stores), plastic-coated wire, floral pruners, wide double-faced satin ribbon

1 Spread wheat on a flat surface. Pick up a few stalks, and hold them in the crux of your hand, just below the grain pods. Add stalks, one at a time and on an angle, to the bunch in your hand, lining up the tips. Move your hand down the bunch as it widens.

2 When all the wheat has been used or you can't hold any more, secure the bunch in the middle with a few tight wraps of plastic-coated wire.

3 Using floral pruners, trim the ends of the stalks so they lie even. Tie a length of ribbon around the waist of the sheaf, allowing the ends to drape.

golden turkey centerpieces

To create a truly showstopping holiday table, go for the gold: Gild resin turkeys with faux gold leaf to make centerpieces. (Metallic floral spray also works well.) It takes about twenty large sheets of gold leaf to cover a large resin turkey and three for a small one. Use the same method and medium if doing multiple projects, since colors and finishes vary. To add a few more Midas touches, top each plate with a gold napkin, folded accordion-style to evoke a turkey with its tail unfurled, then affix it with an embossed golden Dresden ornament.

WHAT YOU WILL NEED Resin turkeys, acrylic paint (in a pale, neutral color), 2 paintbrushes, water-based size adhesive (available at crafts stores), cotton gloves, faux gold leaf, soft-bristle brush, gold dinner napkins, gold twine or ribbon, glue dots, golden Dresden turkey ornaments (available online)

  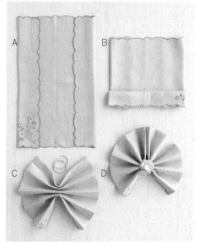

PAINT THE TURKEYS Prime the turkeys with acrylic paint to cover completely. Let dry. Use a second paintbrush to apply water-based size adhesive to turkeys. Let dry.

GILD THE TURKEYS Working in a draft-free room and wearing cotton gloves, lift one gold-leaf sheet from packet. Drape sheet over a turkey, and smooth with fingertips. Use the soft-bristle brush to even out the texture of the gold leaf and remove any flakes. Add another sheet (they should overlap slightly), and smooth. Repeat until the turkey is covered. Touch up any bare spots with adhesive, let dry, then apply gold leaf cut to size. Repeat with remaining turkeys.

FOLD THE NAPKINS Fold the napkin in half lengthwise, and crease. Unfold. Turn 2 sides inward, stopping halfway to the center crease (A). Flip the napkin over. Beginning at an unfolded edge, accordion-fold the napkin at equal intervals (B). Tie the napkin at its center with twine (C). Fan out the folds so the top edges meet and the bottom edges remain apart. Apply a glue dot to the twine, and press the back of the ornament onto it (D).

pomegranates and flowers

A Thanksgiving table demands a feast for the eyes—complete with all the trimmings—
but a well-mannered centerpiece should never block guests' views of one another.
A low container is just what's needed, leaving room for lavish helpings of pomegranates,
red viburnum berries, tulips, roses, and ranunculus surrounded by a bronzy-green
magnolia-leaf border.

WHAT YOU WILL NEED Floral foam block, shallow dish, plastic wrap, knife, floral scissors, magnolia stems, red viburnum berries, tulips, roses, ranunculus, flower picks, pomegranates with stems attached (available at some florists or online)

1 Soak floral foam in water overnight. Line a low, shallow dish with plastic wrap. Trim foam with a knife to fit snugly inside dish, rising about 1 inch above its rim (see above, left; this will help to shape the arrangement into an attractive mound).

2 Trim magnolia stems at a 45-degree angle with floral scissors, and insert them around the foam to form a continuous border.

3 Using floral scissors, cut stems of red viburnum berries, tulips, roses, and ranunculus at 45-degree angles, and insert into foam to create a full mound that conceals the foam.

4 Trim wire of flower picks to 2 inches (use 1 pick for each pomegranate). Twist wire ends around pomegranate stems (see above, right) and insert picks in foam, anchoring firmly. (If pomegranate lacks a stem, insert a pick directly through the flesh of fruit and then insert pick into foam; remove pomegranate from arrangement after a day as juice may leak.) Spritz flowers and foam with water every other day.

CASTING A WARM GLOW

faux-bois candles

Pillar candles in rich gold-and-green faux-bois patterns make a thoroughly modern lighting display. We used six sheets of smooth beeswax to roll a pillar candle from scratch, although you could wrap a sheet of beeswax around a store-bought pillar instead (skip step 1, below). Keep in mind that the color of the sheet of wax may not perfectly match the store-bought candle.

WHAT YOU WILL NEED Ruler, craft knife, smooth beeswax sheets, wicking, kraft paper, 1-inch-wide craft brush, glazing medium (in gold), wood-graining tool, hair dryer (optional)

 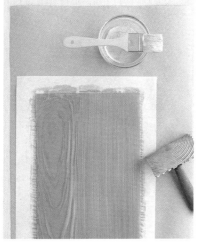 

1 With the ruler and craft knife, cut a sheet of wax to the height you want your candle to be. Cut wicking 1 inch longer than this measurement. Lay wicking along one short edge of the sheet, allowing a ½-inch overhang. Fold the edge of the sheet over the wicking, and roll tightly, adding sheets until candle reaches the desired circumference. Trim. Smooth the seam with your fingertips.

2 With the ruler and craft knife, cut a sheet of wax to fit the just-rolled (or store-bought) candle. Lay the sheet on a flat, clean surface protected with paper. With the craft brush, coat the sheet with the glazing medium. Drag the wood-graining tool across the wax. (If you don't like the results, reapply glazing medium and try again, wiping the wood-graining tool between uses.) Let dry.

3 Align the edges of the glazed sheet with the top and bottom of the candle, and roll the sheet gently in place. The warmth of your fingertips should make it stick; if not, use a hair dryer set on medium to warm it slightly. Smooth out the seam with your fingertips, being careful not to smudge the glaze.

cornhusk votives

Wrapped in dried corn husks, votives cast a soft glow and serve as a reminder that corn was part of the original Thanksgiving menu. For instructions on dyeing dried corn husks, see page 223.

WHAT YOU WILL NEED Cutting mat, ruler, craft knife, dried corn husks (available at specialty grocers), votive holders, double-sided tape, thin ribbon, scissors

On a cutting mat, use a ruler and craft knife to cut the widest part of the dried corn husks to the height of the votive holders. Apply double-sided tape around a votive holder, about a ¼ inch from the bottom. Affix 2 or 3 cut pieces of corn husk, over-lapping the edges, to the holder. Finish by tying with a thin ribbon. (The small vase with roses, pictured below, is also wrapped in corn husks.)

leaf-covered candles

Pillar candles take well to all manner of embellishment and adornments (see page 240 for another example). Here, graceful wax impressions of leaves form a slightly overlapping chain that wraps around the wide circumference of each candle. A group of several such candles makes a striking table display (they would also make a nice hostess gift). Be sure to choose foliage with simple forms, such as lemon, mountain laurel, and rhododendron leaves.

WHAT YOU WILL NEED Four to 6 ounces beeswax, double boiler, crayon (optional, for color), foam craft brush, leaves, pillar candles

Melt beeswax in a double boiler. If you'd like, tint the wax: Mix in ¼-inch pieces of crayon until you achieve the desired shade. (Take note of the ratios you use so you can make more in the same color if needed.) With a foam brush, spread a few thin layers of wax on the back of a leaf, then press the coated side of the leaf firmly onto a pillar candle. Working quickly but carefully, peel back the leaf, leaving a wax impression. Repeat to create a pattern you like.

gourd candles

It's hard to improve upon the shapes found in nature. The squash shells used to mold these candles are perfect examples—with each curve and bump, they capture the essence of the harvest. Use the candles to light an entry hall, or run a length of them down the center of a dining table.

WHAT YOU WILL NEED Acorn squash, paring knife, melon baller, spoon, wax or old candles (to melt down), metal saucepan (preferably with a spout), larger pot, candy thermometer, wicking, wick tabs, wide-mouth glass or jar

1 Remove the stem and enough of the top of an acorn squash to easily fit a melon baller inside. Remove the seeds and pulp. Using a melon baller, scoop out the remaining pulp; work from top to bottom, following the contours of the squash to form hollowed-out tunnels. Smooth the lines between the tunnels with the back of a spoon.

2 Melt the wax or old candles in a metal saucepan that is set over, but not touching, a pot of boiling water, until the thermometer registers 180°F. As the wax is heating, cut a piece of wicking 3 inches longer than the height of the squash, and attach a metal wick tab to the bottom. Carefully pour the wax into the squash (steady it, if necessary, in a wide-mouthed glass or jar). Holding the top of the wick, drop the metal tab into the squash; it will sink. Tie wick to spoon and rest on squash to set. Trim the wick 2 inches above the surface of the wax.

3 Let the squash sit until it is cool to the touch, 4 to 5 hours (if the center sinks, fill it with more hot wax). When cooled, the squash skin should peel away easily, leaving a patina on the wax. To even the candle's bottom (so it sits upright), carve with a knife, or heat a knife and rub its blade along the bottom.

paper pilgrim hat and bonnet

Easily crafted with a few folds, paper hats and bonnets help kids get into character as Pilgrims. You can cut the pieces, and let the kids do the gluing and tying.

WHAT YOU WILL NEED Pilgrim hat and buckle template (see page 358), pencil, drawing paper (in dark gray), metallic paper (in gold), scissors, glue dots, 11-by-17 heavy-stock paper, seam binding, ruler, hole punch

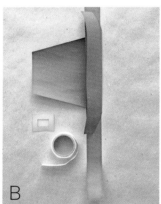

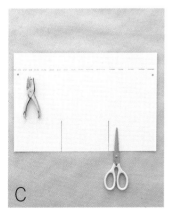

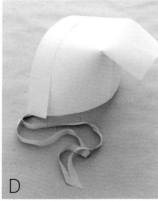

FOR THE HAT Download and print the template for the hat and buckle, and trace them onto drawing paper (A). Cut out the buckle from metallic gold paper. Cut out the silhouette of the hat, then fold up the brim. Cut out the headband; rest it inside the fold of the brim, and secure with a glue dot (B). Glue buckle onto hat, above brim. Wrap headband around head, and secure with a glue dot (or tape).

FOR THE BONNET Use an 11-by-17-inch piece of heavy-stock paper and two 24-inch lengths of seam binding. Mark 1½ inches from the top edge of the paper, then use a ruler to draw a dotted fold line. Use the hole punch to make a hole on each side, ½ inch beneath the fold line and ½ inch from the edge. Mark spots 5½ inches from each bottom edge, then make a 3-inch vertical cut line from each point (C). Fold across dotted line to make a cuff; thread seam binding through each hole. Fold bottom corners inward to create back of bonnet and secure with glue dots; fold down back flap and secure with glue dots (D).

paper-sail centerpiece

Everyone looks forward to Thanksgiving, but sitting through a long meal can be a challenge for children. A specially decorated kids' table will help encourage a pleasant gathering for everyone. Making this centerpiece is a breeze: A sheet of torn-edged watercolor paper becomes the main sail, and a blue burlap tablecloth replicates the ocean. Fill a bucket with rolled-up bonnets and hats (page 247) and place on the table.

WHAT YOU WILL NEED Three wooden dowels (one ½-inch wide; two ¼-inch wide), watercolor paper, metal ruler, construction paper, twine, hole punch, scissors, white craft glue, bucket, pebbles

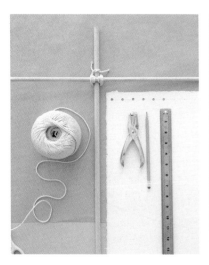 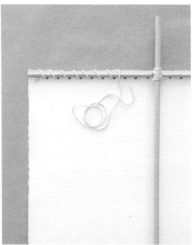

1 Cut the ½-inch wooden dowel 40 inches long (for the mast) and each ¼-inch wooden dowel 23 inches long (for the crossbars). Cut a 22-inch square piece of watercolor paper (tear along a metal ruler to create a deckle edge), and a triangular piece of construction paper for the flag. Using twine, attach the top crossbar to the mast, 5 inches from the top (secure with a tight double knot). Center the sail underneath the mast on a table. Mark and then punch holes at 1-inch intervals. Repeat for bottom edge.

2 Cut a 1-yard length of twine, and thread, whipstitch-style, through holes and around crossbar. Knot at ends, and trim excess. Attach bottom crossbar 19 inches below top crossbar. Thread twine again to connect sail to bottom crossbar. Glue flag to top of mast. Anchor mast in a bucket weighted with pebbles.

pom-pom toms

Kids and adults alike will delight in this quirky flock of yarn-and-felt birds. They're perfect for holding place cards or hanging out in the center of the table. You'll need some yarn, a few basic crafts-store supplies, and a couple of pom-pom makers—a larger one for the body and a smaller one for the head. For basic instructions on making pom-poms, see page 342. You can also create orange pom-pom pumpkins and embellish them with green felt leaves.

WHAT YOU WILL NEED Pom-pom maker kit (with several sizes; available at crafts and knitting stores), wool yarn (in red, brown, gray, yellow, and white), small scissors, waxed twine (in red and brown), yarn needle, white and black embroidery floss, pom-pom toms template (see page 358), medium-size sewing needle, disappearing-ink fabric pen, wool felt (in black, red, white, brown, and gold), hot-glue gun, black pipe cleaners or heavy floral wire

1 Make pom-poms as described on page 342: You'll need one 1¼-inch red pom-pom for the head, and one 2³⁄₁₆-inch brown pom-pom for the body. Tie pom-pom halves together in center with waxed twine. Trim pom-poms so that the yarn is even all around.

2 To make the wings, thread a yarn needle with a long doubled piece of white, yellow, and/or gray yarn. Keeping loose ends aligned, push it through the body pom-pom, leaving excess yarn on both sides; thread back through. Repeat until wings reach desired size and shape, using multiple colors if you like. Cut needle free; trim yarn flush. Repeat this technique for eyes on red pom-pom, using white and then black floss.

3 Download and print turkey tail template (enlarging as desired for bigger birds), and cut out. With a disappearing-ink pen, trace onto several colors of felt; cut out. Stack, in descending size order, then hot-glue to secure; hold until glue is set, about 30 seconds.

4 Apply a generous amount of glue to base of tail feathers, and attach to body; hold in place 1 minute. Repeat to affix head to body. Download, print, and cut out wattle templates.

Trace onto red felt; cut out. Apply glue to top edges, part yarn at base of head, and insert the two shapes, the smaller one above the larger one. Hold in place 30 seconds. Download, print, and cut out beak template; trace it onto gold felt, and cut out. Apply a dab of glue to the base of each piece, and use a needle to help attach to head; hold in place 30 seconds.

5 To make legs, cut two 3-inch pieces and two 1¾-inch pieces of pipe cleaner (for larger birds, use heavy floral wire). Fold a 3-inch pipe cleaner 1 inch from end; adjust longer side so it's perpendicular, with a ½-inch crimp at the back of the foot. Fold a 1¾-inch piece of pipe cleaner into a V shape; dab glue on outside corner, and slide inside crimped edge. Hold in place 30 seconds. Repeat with remaining pieces of pipe cleaner to make the other leg.

6 Apply glue to tops of legs and insert into body as far as they will go; hold in place 30 seconds. Set turkeys on their backs to dry for 10 minutes before displaying upright. Once you've completed a turkey, give him one final trim to ensure his furry feathers are even. In general, the closer you cut the yarn, the denser the pom-pom will be.

turkey trot centerpiece

Set out a family of chocolate turkeys to parade across the table. Children especially will enjoy the spectacle, and will look forward to taking the birds home as favors once dinner is over.

WHAT YOU WILL NEED Ruler, pencil, card stock, scissors, pinking or scalloping shears, hole punch, bone folder, ¼-inch grosgrain ribbon, hay or straw, foil-wrapped chocolate turkeys (1 large and several small), wheat stalks, pen, hot-glue gun

Use a ruler and pencil to mark a 1-inch border on an 11-by-6-inch piece of card stock. Trim edges with pinking shears. With scissors, cut a 1-inch square from each corner. Punch two holes in each flap at corners. Fold flaps inward to create a box, creasing with a bone folder. Tie a short piece of ribbon through the two holes at each corner and knot. Line box with hay or straw and nestle turkeys inside. Bundle several stalks of wheat together, and tie with ribbon. Inscribe a label on a scrap of card stock; hot-glue to wheat.

turkey trivia

Encourage the children at the table to talk turkey with a flock of entertaining place cards.
Download and print the turkey trivia templates (see page 359) and trace onto heavyweight
paper; cut out. Write a turkey-themed question on one side of each feather, the answer on the
other. Punch a hole through each feather and the body. Stack 5 feathers per bird, questions
forward; secure to body with a paper fastener. Fan out the feathers. Write a guest's name on
each body. To stand, cut a 1½-inch slit in the bottom of the body. Cut a 1½-inch half circle
from heavyweight paper; insert circular edge in slit.

It's the festival of lights: For eight nights, candles are illuminated, presents are exchanged, and an ancient miracle is quietly, joyously heralded. You may be wrapping gelt, making a simple toy for a child, or setting the table for a holiday meal. In every case, the objects that have become symbolic of Hanukkah—the dreidel, the menorah, the Star of David—can take center stage. Gather decorative papers and ribbons in shades of blue, and glitter in silver and gold. Use them, along with a few crafters' tricks, to transform ordinary materials into the icons of a glowing holiday. Our Hanukkah crafts feature lots of ideas for packaging **GIFTS AND GELT**, including beautifully wrapped presents, glittered dreidel toppers, and gorgeous bows in the signature blue-and-silver palette. We've also included some of our best-loved ideas for menorahs and tabletop candles in a section fittingly titled **A CELEBRATION OF LIGHT**; in it you'll find star-patterned punch paper designs to wrap around glass hurricane lanterns, a nature-inspired menorah made of a large tree branch, and more.

PREVIOUS Glittered Dreidels, see page 258 for how-to

GIFTS AND GELT

WRAPPED GELT Give Hanukkah gelt a smart wrapping treatment. Wrap small metal canisters with decorative paper and fill with coins. To create the paper sleeve, download and print the wrapped dreidel template (see page 359) to desired size. Trace onto wrapping paper and cut out with a craft knife. Affix to metal canister with double-sided tape. Use a round label to create a name tag for the top. Alternatively, wrap a stack of coins in crepe paper. Tie each end with ribbon. Finish with a paper sleeve decorated with a menorah craft punch (available online).

glittered dreidels

Transform plain wooden dreidels into dazzling holiday decorations with a coat of fine glitter. For an easy holiday centerpiece, place several in a clear glass jar (see photograph on page 254). You can also add a pony bead to the top of each and string them into a shimmering garland, or use individually as gift toppers. Use varying sizes of dreidels and different shades of glitter for a sparkling effect.

WHAT YOU WILL NEED Plain wooden dreidels, white craft glue, paintbrush, paper plate, fine glitter, small bowl, spoon, large glass containers, quick-bonding cement or glue, pony beads, thin strand of lametta tinsel, satin ribbon

FOR CENTERPIECE Holding each dreidel by its handle, brush all but one side with glue. Pour glitter in a small bowl. Use a spoon to sprinkle the dreidel with glitter while holding it over a paper plate. Let dreidel rest on plain side while glue dries. Once dry, glue and glitter plain side of dreidel and handle; let dry. Arrange dreidels in large glass containers.

FOR GARLANDS AND GIFT TOPPERS
Working in a well-ventilated area, use the bonding cement to attach a pony bead (or other large bead with a hole) to the top of each plain dreidel; let dry. Cover dreidels with glitter, following instructions for the centerpiece (left). Make a garland by threading a long strand of lametta tinsel through the beads, spacing dreidels evenly (the tinsel's fringe will keep the dreidels from sliding). Or, for a topper, thread a strand of ribbon through the bead and wrap it around a gift (as shown, above right).

dreidel gift-card holders

Brighten up a gift card by presenting it in a personalized dreidel-shaped holder. Download and print the dreidel template (see page 359) onto patterned card stock, enlarging as desired; you'll need two pieces for each card holder. Cut out. For a front-pocket card: Lightly brush one dreidel cutout with white craft glue. Sprinkle with clear glitter; let dry. With a craft knife, cut a slit along dotted line. Brush glue onto edges of second dreidel. Top with glittered dreidel; let dry. For a pocket card: Stack two dreidels. Sew edges together, leaving top open. Lightly brush one side with glue. Sprinkle with glitter; let dry. Finish with a thin ribbon tied around the center.

curling ribbons

A few twists and turns can transform ordinary, dime-store ribbons into something extraordinary. Concentric loops and long teardrop shapes impart a modern look. Accordion folds make a flower or a lone sunburst rendered in ribbon. Bend wide ribbons (which hold their shape) into a geometric medley, or repeat one shape for a bold statement.

WHAT YOU WILL NEED Decorative ribbon, stapler, scissors, double-sided tape, needle and thread

FORMING CONCENTRIC CIRCLES

FORMING TEARDROP

STAPLING TO SECURE

FORMING FOLDED FLOWERS AND SUNBURSTS

FOR A CONCENTRIC DESIGN Make small circles, then larger ones, working from the spool and holding the ribbon at the bottom.

FOR TEARDROPS Hold the ribbon in the middle and loop to either side.

FOR BOTH CONCENTRIC AND TEARDROP SHAPES Staple at the bottom (use a mini stapler if a larger one won't fit); trim end of ribbon. Affix to a gift with double-sided tape, hiding staples with the loops of more ribbons.

TO MAKE FOLDED FLOWERS AND SUNBURSTS Accordion-fold ribbon from the spool in equal lengths (3 to 5 inches), making 27 points (14 on one side, 13 on the other). Stack folds; use a needle to pull a piece of thread through the stack at the bottom (where the loose ends are). Knot the thread loosely and cut. Open folds into a circle, or for a fuller look, use double-sided tape to connect 2 half circles.

ribbon star of david

It's easy to form ribbon into six-pointed stars. In shades of blue and silver, the stars make lovely toppers for Hanukkah gifts. We also used them atop the favors shown on page 269. For best results, use stiff ribbon, such as grosgrain or metallic braid. The wider the ribbon, the bigger the star.

WHAT YOU WILL NEED One-inch-wide stiff ribbon, scissors, disappearing-ink fabric pen, hot-glue gun, white craft glue

1 Cut 1-inch-wide ribbon into two 17-inch lengths. If using wider or narrower ribbon, alter length to keep a 1-to-17 proportion; substitute 1 ribbon width for each inch in step 2.

2 Lay one ribbon vertically. Measure 1 inch from top; mark on right edge with a disappearing-ink fabric pen. Mark again 4 inches below first dot; mark a third dot 4 inches below that. With disappearing-ink pen, extend each mark into an equilateral triangle (A).

3 Starting at top, fold ribbon along first marked triangle; using a hot-glue gun, glue beneath fold to secure.

4 Repeat at next 2 marked triangles (B), folding top end first and gluing bottom-end fold. Trim ribbon even with side of resulting triangle; tuck under first point.

5 With second ribbon, repeat steps 2 and 3.

6 Weave folded point of second ribbon under left side of completed triangle, over right side (C). With disappearing-ink pen, mark top point of triangle for orientation.

7 Fold ribbon at second marked triangle. Weave ribbon under bottom side of triangle. Fold ribbon at third marked triangle. Weave ribbon under lower-right point of triangle (D). Trim ribbon; tuck under upper-right point.

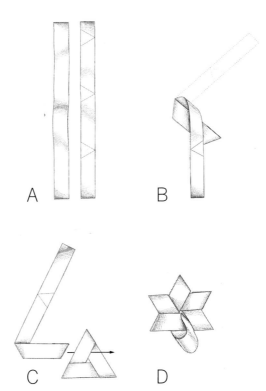

A

B

C

D

hanukkah gift-wrapping ideas

Take time to wrap a gift thoughtfully, and it will feel all the more special to the lucky person who gets to open it. These ideas can be adapted to suit nearly any holiday, using other pop-up shapes and papers in a different palette.

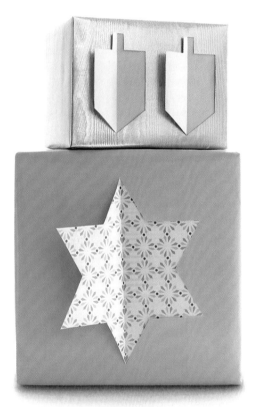

pop-up symbols

Dress up Hanukkah gifts with holiday cutouts while also playing patterns against solid colors. For the star: Wrap package in patterned paper. Fold blue paper around it, leaving impressions where corners will be. Using a glue stick, affix more patterned paper to the blue paper, wrong sides facing. Download and print the half-star template (see page 359) onto card stock and cut out. Outline a half star on the blue paper. Cut out with a craft knife; fold to crease. Wrap package, blue side out; center star. For the dreidels: Follow directions above, but use the dreidel template to make two cutouts, and reverse solid and patterned papers.

snowflake toppers

White paper doilies conjure images of snowflakes; silver doilies are especially appropriate for Hanukkah. Pair with pale blue and silver wrapping paper to create an irresistible package. If you like, snip around the doily's edges to create patterns. Thread a ribbon through the holes of one or more doilies (depending on the size of the box). Wrap the ribbon around the box and affix with double-sided tape. If using a wide ribbon, cut a slit in the center of the doily to thread the ribbon through.

gelt favor boxes

*Chocolate coins wrapped in silver foil make charming favors when presented
in clip-art card stock boxes tied with ribbon and sealed with a Star of David.*

WHAT YOU WILL NEED Gelt favor box clip art (see page 359), matte heavyweight paper,
scissors, bone folder, ruler, gelt (foil-wrapped chocolate coins), Star of David craft punch,
silver paper, narrow satin ribbon, double-sided tape

Download and print clip art onto the heavyweight paper; cut out. Score along dotted lines with
the bone folder. For straight lines, use a ruler for guidance. Fold box, first along straight lines,
then on one end to close. Fill box with gelt. Close open end. Using the craft punch, punch out
a star from silver paper. Wrap ribbon around box and secure with a star using double-sided
tape. Trim ends of ribbon.

A CELEBRATION OF LIGHT

star-punched hurricane lamps

On this stylish and elegant tablescape, hurricane vases and votive candle-holders are wrapped in star-punched paper—an easy way to suffuse a holiday dinner with warmth. Download and print the star-punched hurricane templates (see page 359), enlarging as needed. Cut decorative paper so it's flush with the top of the hurricane vase and the paper ends overlap by about ½ inch. Lay template over decorative paper on a cutting mat. Punch the pattern through both papers with a screw punch. Wrap paper around hurricane vase and secure with double-sided tape.

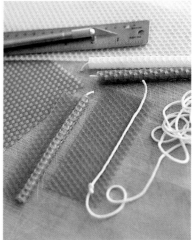

hand-rolled hanukkah candles

During the eight days of Hanukkah, a total of forty-four candles are lit. Hand-rolled candles, made from sheets of beeswax in the subtlest shades of ivory, butter yellow, and deep olive, cast a warm glow on any setting—and give off a lovely, very subtle scent as well. Make a set for yourself, and more to serve as holiday gifts.

WHAT YOU WILL NEED Craft knife, ruler, beeswax sheets (available at crafts stores and online), wicking, hair dryer

Using the craft knife and ruler, slice wax sheets into 2½-by-6-inch rectangles. Cut wicking into 7-inch lengths; make a knot close to one end. Warm wax with a hair dryer until just pliable, 10 to 15 seconds. Lay wicking along edge of wax with ¾ inch of wick hanging beyond wax. Tightly roll wax around wicking; press seam with your finger to smooth and seal.

manzanita-branch menorah

Set a nature-inspired table with a menorah made from a Manzanita branch.
The branch is covered with shimmering silver floral spray and trimmed with candle
clips adorned with blue vellum stars. In keeping with holiday tradition, a small gift
awaits each guest. But what's inside each box (topped with a ribbon star; see page
263 for instructions) is not the only surprise: Hidden within each folded napkin is
chocolate gelt. See page 224 for instructions on the envelope napkin fold.

WHAT YOU WILL NEED Manzanita branch (available at crafts and florist-supply stores),
silver floral spray, candle clips, Manzanita-branch menorah star template (see page 359),
card stock, pencil, craft knife, blue vellum, ½-inch circle craft punch, Hanukkah candles

1 Working in a well-ventilated area, on a covered surface, coat the Manzanita branch completely with silver floral spray. Let dry.

2 Attach 9 candle clips along branch, with one higher than the rest (for the shammes candle).

3 Download and print the star template onto card stock. Using the craft knife, cut out. With a pencil, trace the template 9 times onto blue vellum. Cut out.

4 Using the ½-inch circle punch, remove center of each star. Cut a slit from one indented point of star to circle center. Slide stars onto clips. Insert a Hanukkah candle into each.

kids' glittered menorah

Here's a fun and easy project to do with kids. It makes good use of accessible household materials—a plain piece of wood, some glue, ¼-inch metal nuts, and glitter— and serves as a helpful way to teach about the significance of the menorah as you craft together. Line a silver tray with wrapping paper and place the finished menorah in the center of the table to give your handiwork pride of place.

WHAT YOU WILL NEED One piece of wood (cut to about 8 by 1⅝ by ¾ inches), wood glue, ten ¼-inch nuts, kraft paper, white craft glue, paintbrush, fine glitter (in silver and blue), small bowls, spoon, toothpicks, candles

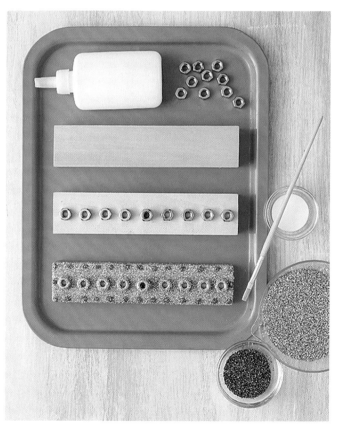

1 Using wood glue, attach 10 nuts to the wooden base: a stack of 2 in the middle (for the shammes candle), with 4 evenly spaced on either side. Let dry.

2 Cover your work surface with kraft paper. Brush all but the underside of the base with white craft glue. Working over a bowl, spoon on silver glitter to cover completely; let dry.

3 To add colored details, use a toothpick to dot the edges of the base with glue and sprinkle with blue glitter.

4 Once the glue dries, insert the candles in the menorah.

Christmas

When you think back on your childhood holidays, often what comes to mind as much as the toys you received are the crafts you made. Chances are you created ornaments or garlands for the tree, or tied tags or toppers or bows to wrapped gifts, or even helped set the table in its once-a-year finery. What you'll discover as you conjure up images of your own Christmases past is that it's the process of making things by hand that most embodies "getting into the holiday spirit." This is, in fact, the crafter's lucky point of view. We've collected our best-ever Christmas content, including ideas for **TREE TRIMMINGS** that make the most of ribbons, rickrack, beads, and other household materials, along with all of the basics on proper Christmas tree care. You'll find decorating projects to inspire you as you **DECK THE HALLS**, along with **GREAT WREATHS** and ideas to help create **A FESTIVE TABLE** for entertaining. Handmade cards appear in **SEASON'S GREETINGS**, and sweet, simple, easy-to-make tokens will encourage you to **GIVE CHEER**. Finally, we offer **TIES, TAGS, AND TOPPERS** to help provide the perfect finishing touches to your thoughtful gifts.

PREVIOUS Ribbon Ornaments, see pages 276 to 278 for how-to

TREE TRIMMINGS

RICKRACK ORNAMENTS
Snippets of rickrack and ribbon can be fashioned into homespun ornaments. For candy canes and wreaths, twist pieces of rickrack together, shape, iron flat, and set with fabric stiffener; adorn with tiny bows, poinsettias, or holly made of ribbon or trim. For how-to, see page 279.

looped and gathered ribbon ornaments

The tabletop tree on page 272 is trimmed largely with easy-to-assemble ribbon ornaments. Crisscrossed figure-eight bows and petal bows spin like snowflakes; layered-loop bows, hung vertically, mimic ribbon candy.

WHAT YOU WILL NEED Stiff satin ribbon (⅜- and ⅝-inch-wide), scissors, white craft glue, silver twine, needle and thread, small paintbrush, fabric glue

FOR FIGURE EIGHT Form a loop at one end of a 15-inch length of ⅜-inch-wide satin ribbon; glue in place. Wind the rest of the ribbon back and forth, forming a figure eight; form another figure eight, making it a little larger than the one before. Glue in center point to secure. Make two more bows of double figure eights. Cross and glue two of the bows. Glue a loop of silver twine at the front center. Glue the third bow across the middle, as shown, concealing the twine.

FOR PETAL BOW RIBBON Make 2¼-inch accordion folds in ribbon (the one shown is ⅝ inch wide and 45 inches long), holding the folds in place with your fingers as you work. End with cut edges on the same side. Pass a needle and thread through that end, about ¼ inch from edge. Hold together, and pull thread taut; knot. Fan petals; tie a loop of silver twine around thread to make a hanger.

FOR LAYERED LOOP Make 2 layered-loop stacks from ⅝-inch-wide satin ribbon: Bend two 8-inch ribbons into circles, attaching ends with fabric glue. Repeat with two 6-inch ribbons. Pinch each circle together at center; secure with a dab of glue. For the smallest loops, wrap a piece of ribbon around your thumb; glue ends together. Repeat. Stack loops as pictured; glue together. Fold an 8-inch piece of silver twine in half. With a paintbrush, apply glue to undersides of both tacks; press together, sandwiching ends of silver twine inside. Wrap ribbon around center of stacks; secure with glue, concealing ends inside a loop.

candy-basket ornaments

Fill sturdy paper "baskets" with peppermints or other small candies and dangle them from the tree branches. Choose card stock and ribbons in complementary colors for a visually appealing display.

WHAT YOU WILL NEED Candy-basket template (see page 359), card stock, scissors, ruler, bone folder, white craft glue, small paintbrush, bowl, clear glitter, ¼-inch-wide ribbon, mini paper fasteners, fabric glue, candy

1 Download and print template onto card stock; cut along solid lines. Score along dotted lines using a ruler and bone folder. Fold inward along innermost lines to form basket's sides; fold outward along outer lines to create a rim. Overlap sides slightly, and secure by applying craft glue with a paintbrush; hold until set (as shown above). Brush glue on outside of basket. Working over a bowl, spoon glitter over glue, covering completely. Let dry; repeat on inside.

2 When basket is dry, lay it facedown, and crisscross three 14-inch lengths of ¼-inch-wide ribbon (as shown above). Attach ribbons to basket at center with a mini paper fastener. With same kind of ribbon, make two 2¼-inch-long tuxedo bows: Fold ends of one piece of ribbon in toward the center, overlapping to form a loop; secure with fabric glue. Flatten at center and secure with fabric glue. Cover center with a second piece of ribbon, gluing at back of bow; repeat to make a second bow. Cut another 7-inch strip of ribbon for hanging the ornament.

3 Turn basket right-side up, and gather ribbon ends together so they lie flat against each other at the top of a triangle. Cut off any excess, and then dab fabric glue along top of cut ends to secure; hold until it sets (as shown above). Glue the inner side of each end of the 7-inch hanging-ribbon strip to one flat side of the gathered cut ends, making a loop. Glue a tiny tuxedo bow to each side to conceal ribbon ends. Fill basket with candy.

ribbon medallion tree trimmings

Pleating grosgrain ribbon results in a pinwheel shape that is intricate but sturdy.
Make several to hang as ornaments on the tree, and a larger one to serve as the topper.
The technique works for satin ribbon, as well.

WHAT YOU WILL NEED Scissors, grosgrain ribbon (we used red-and-white striped), needle and thread, white craft glue, small paintbrush, silver twine

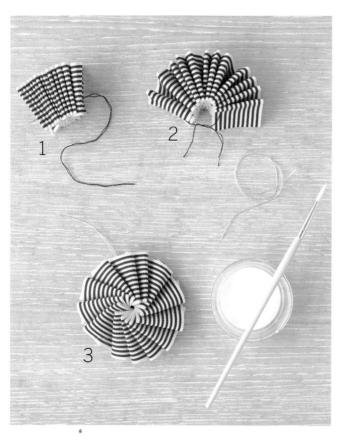

1 Make 1-inch accordion folds in 1 yard of grosgrain ribbon, holding the folds in place as you work. Finish with cut ends of ribbon on the same side. Thread a needle, leaving a 1-inch thread tail beyond the knot. Pass the needle and thread through the layers near the ribbon's cut ends, about ¼ inch from the edge.

2 Bring ends of thread together; knot, close to ribbon. Cut off excess thread. Attach the two ends of the ribbon with craft glue, covering the knot. Fan folds so they're evenly spaced.

3 Press the center of the medallion to flatten, rotating the folds in one direction. Thread silver twine through the center; knot to make hanger.

rickrack ornaments

You can weave rickrack into decorative braids, gather it with a needle and thread
to fashion flowers, or stiffen it to create wreaths, holly clusters, and candy canes.
Loop ornaments with silver thread to hang.

WHAT YOU WILL NEED Rickrack (in a variety of colors and widths), embroidery scissors, fabric glue, iron, corrugated cardboard and clear packing tape, straight pins, paintbrush, fabric stiffener, silver thread, needle and thread, "pips" (artificial stamens available at craft stores)

TWISTING Twisted trim is used to fashion candy cane and wreath ornaments and embellishments. Because of rickrack's wavy weave, two pieces can be made into a single strand with interlocking points. Cut two equal lengths of a single color, or, for a candy-stripe effect, one in each of two hues. Affix pieces at one end with fabric glue; let dry. Intertwine the two pieces. The result will look bumpy; press with a steam iron on high heat. Snip the ends evenly, and glue them together. Allow to dry.

SHAPING AND STIFFENING Cover a piece of corrugated cardboard with clear packing tape to prevent stiffened rickrack from sticking to the surface. With your fingers, shape finished lengths of rickrack twists into circle, candy cane, or holly leaf shapes, using pins to hold in place on the board. With a small paintbrush, generously coat ornament with fabric stiffener, which is white when wet. Let dry (it will dry clear). Loop silver thread through and tie ends together.

GATHERING Oversize rickrack is hand-gathered into larger poinsettias with floral-wire pips in the centers; the wider the rickrack is, the bigger the flower will be. Cut a 13-point piece of rickrack. We used contrasting thread to demonstrate, but you should use a matching color. Baste and tightly gather points on one side of trim, and knot (A); without cutting thread, sew folded ends together with a running stitch (B), and glue to prevent fraying. Snip pips from ends of wire; attach to center of each flower with fabric glue.

holiday card ornaments

These ornamental balls are made from holiday cards saved from Christmases past. Vary the size of the balls by cutting circles in graduated sizes; you will need twenty for each ornament. For convenience, use circle punches, available at crafts stores and online.

WHAT YOU WILL NEED Holiday cards, 1¼-inch circle punch, drinking glass, scissors, cardboard, bone folder, ruler, white craft glue, paintbrush, silver cord

Cut out 20 circles: For a small ball, use a 1¼-inch circle punch; for a large one, trace around the bottom of a glass (or use a larger punch). Cut one more circle from cardboard; draw an equilateral triangle, points touching the circumference. Cut out triangle; trace it onto the inside of each circle. Score and fold along all the lines. Next, use craft glue to join one flap from each of 2 circles; triangles should point in the same direction. Using the same technique, attach 3 more circles to these 2, forming what will be the top. Make the bottom the same way. Glue remaining 10 circles together, triangle points alternating up and down, forming a line. Glue 2 end flaps to form what will be the middle section; then glue top and bottom to its flaps. Let dry, then hang from a loop of silver cord.

cookie cutter ornaments

With inexpensive aluminum cookie cutters, you can turn out ornaments faster than you can bake a batch of treats. Choose patterned papers or designs cut from vintage cards, or print favorite family photographs onto card stock.

WHAT YOU WILL NEED Patterned paper or heavyweight photo paper and photos, pencil, aluminum cookie cutters, scissors, small paintbrush, white craft glue, needle, narrow ribbon, beads

If you are using family photos, download and print images onto photo paper. Trace a cookie cutter onto patterned paper or card stock, and cut out. Using a paintbrush, dab craft glue along the cutter's edge. Press paper in place; let dry. Thread a narrow ribbon through the eye of a needle, then poke needle between paper and cutter. Wrap ribbon around top of cutter, and slip a bead over ribbon's ends. Tie a knot to form a loop for hanging.

gilded harvest tree

In Poland and other parts of Central and Eastern Europe, where the Christmas season
is seen as a time of renewal, traditional ornaments are fashioned from straw to symbolize
thanksgiving for the harvest and hope for good things in the coming year. Eggs represent
the promise of future prosperity, too. On this Polish-inspired tree, egg ornaments gilded
with mica powders in a range of hues, from light copper to a deep verdigris, mingle with
gold glass balls and handmade wheat decorations, also burnished with gold mica powders.
For the instructions, see pages 284 and 285.

gilded egg ornaments

Painted eggs are used as ornaments and other decorations at Christmas (and Easter, of course) in many parts of the world, particularly Poland and Ukraine; these quail and chicken eggs glimmer, thanks to a coat of mica powder. White latex enamel is used to create decorative details and flourishes on each gilded base.

WHAT YOU WILL NEED Long pin or craft knife, chicken or quail eggs, aspirator, small paintbrush, water-based size adhesive (see note below), soft artist's brush, mica powder, dust mask, rubber band, small pointed paintbrush, off-white latex enamel paint, white craft glue, foil paper trim (available online), beads, model cement, thin gold cord

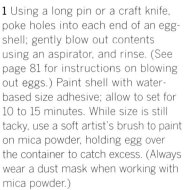

water-based size adhesive

Size is used to apply gilding leaf or mica powder to wood or other surfaces. Like paint, size can be oil- or water-based. While oil-based size gives the leaf a shinier, more luminescent appearance, it is also more toxic and is therefore used most often for outdoor applications. Water-based size is preferred for the projects in this book. The size is white and can be used for all colors of gilding leaf or mica powder. Before applying gilding leaf or mica powder, let the size set and become tacky, per the manufacturer's instructions.

1 Using a long pin or a craft knife, poke holes into each end of an eggshell; gently blow out contents using an aspirator, and rinse. (See page 81 for instructions on blowing out eggs.) Paint shell with water-based size adhesive; allow to set for 10 to 15 minutes. While size is still tacky, use a soft artist's brush to paint on mica powder, holding egg over the container to catch excess. (Always wear a dust mask when working with mica powder.)

2 Place a rubber band around middle of shell as a guide, and use a small pointed paintbrush dipped in latex enamel paint to apply designs. Let dry completely. Glue foil-paper trim and beads on each end of egg. Affix beads with model cement. Thread gold cord through top bead to hang.

burnished straw ornaments

Strands of wheat and straw are crafted into ornaments in four configurations for the Polish-inspired tree on page 282. Stems of wheat are clustered in graceful sheaves or tied to make simple geometric stars; tiny braided and wired wreaths represent traditional ring-shaped Christmas decorations. All are burnished with mica powder for a golden glow.

WHAT YOU WILL NEED Triticum and arrow wheat, 28-gauge gold wire, scissors, 18-gauge gold wire, thin ribbon, transparent tape, gold cord (thick and thin), hot-glue gun, iron, white craft glue, water-based size adhesive (see note, opposite), wide soft paintbrush, mica powder, dust mask

WHEAT BUNCH

WIRED WREATH

BRAIDED WREATH

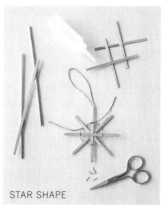

STAR SHAPE

FOR WHEAT BUNCH Wire three 6-inch strands of triticum wheat together 1 inch from stem ends using 28-gauge wire; separate and shape wheat. Make hanger by tying 18-gauge wire where strands are tied together. Finish by tying a decorative bow made from thin ribbon over wire.

FOR WIRED WREATH Make a wreath form by shaping 18-gauge wire into a circle 2 to 3 inches in diameter; tape ends together to close. Tie thick cord into a circle. Loop it around itself on the form to make a hanger. Cut the arrow wheat tips and hot-glue them, slightly overlapping, to both sides of the form.

FOR BRAIDED WREATH Soak six 10- to 12-inch pieces of arrow wheat overnight, then wire together ½ inch below tips. Divide stems into 3 sets of 2, and braid. Pull braid around to form a circle, and wrap 28-gauge wire at the same spot as other wire. Grasping 3 tips in each hand, pull in opposite directions to finish.

FOR STAR SHAPE Cut 4 equal-length stems of triticum or arrow wheat. Soak in water overnight. Iron flat, using steam setting. Affix pairs of stems in X shapes with craft glue. Stack X shapes, alternating stems; glue. Wrap thin gold cord once around stems, weaving over and under; glue in place. Cut stem tips into points or V shapes; hot-glue a loop of cord inside tip of one stem to hang.

TO BURNISH ALL ORNAMENTS Brush ornaments with water-based size. Let set 10 to 15 minutes, until tacky. Use a wide, soft paintbrush to apply mica powder, working over tin to catch excess. (Always wear a dust mask when working with mica powder.) Hot-glue small ribbon bows to ornaments.

cinnamon bird ornaments

Create a woodland-themed Christmas tree with a flock of colorful birds, each adorned with markings inspired by nature or your imagination. Though these whimsical holiday-scented birds look and smell like gingerbread cookies, their sparkling, beaded plumage hints at their true nature as sweet works of art. Applesauce gives the dough pliability, glue makes it firm (and inedible), and cinnamon imparts a lovely fragrance and color. Once dried and decorated, the ornaments should last for many Christmases to come.

WHAT YOU WILL NEED Bowls, ground cinnamon, applesauce, rubber spatula, white craft glue, rolling pin, cinnamon bird ornament templates (see page 359) or bird-shaped cookie cutters, scissors, hole punch, craft knife, drinking straw, wire rack and paper towels or baking sheet, applicator bottle and tip, glitter, beads, thin ribbon, tissue paper

1 In a medium bowl, mix together 1 cup ground cinnamon and ¼ cup applesauce using a rubber spatula. Add ½ cup craft glue; stir until dough is smooth and dry. Let stand 1 hour. Turn out one-quarter of dough onto a cool, flat surface; flatten with your hands, then with a rolling pin to ¼-inch thickness. If dough becomes too dry, spritz with water. If it sticks to rolling pin or work surface, sprinkle with additional cinnamon.

2 Download and print templates onto card stock: cut out, punching holes where indicated. Lay a template over the dough; cut out shape with a craft knife (or use cookie cutters). Repeat with remaining quarters of dough. With a straw, poke a hole in dough as indicated on template (for hanging). Air-dry ornaments on a wire rack lined with paper towels for 24 hours, flipping every 6 hours or so to keep them flat. Alternatively, bake on a cookie sheet at 200°F, flipping once, until dry, about 2 hours.

3 To decorate, proceed from finest embellishment to the coarsest, adding glitter, then beads in order of size: Using the applicator bottle and tip, spread glue over the area you wish to decorate, using the markings on the templates as a guide, if desired. While glue is still wet, sprinkle with glitter or beads, holding ornament over a bowl; tap off excess.

4 Wait for the first area to dry completely (at least 30 minutes) before glittering or beading another section. Thread a length of thin ribbon through ornament's hole, trim the ends to prevent fraying, and knot. (Store ornaments, wrapped individually in tissue paper, in a cool, dry place.)

beaded candy cane ornaments

Beaded striped candy canes are a good introduction to working with beads. Transferring beads to wires takes a little time, but twisting them into shape is a joy. The ornaments are even more dazzling in multiples. The characteristic red-and-white color scheme is one option, but you can use any color or combinations of colors of beads, such as the green and blue ones shown.

WHAT YOU WILL NEED 24-gauge tinned copper wire, wire cutters, round-nose pliers, strands of rocaille and tri-cut beads (buy them in hanks), masking tape

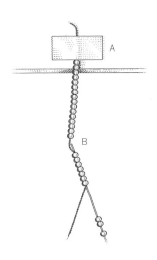

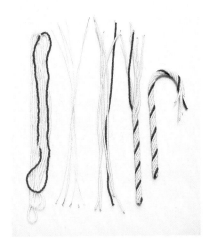

1 Choose a color combination: A four-strand candy cane in red, green, and white, for instance, will be composed of two wires with white beads, one wire with green beads, and one wire with red beads. A six-strand candy cane with those colors has four wires with white beads, one wire with green beads, and one wire with red beads. A five-strand cane in red and white has four wires with white beads and one wire with red beads. Use only one kind of bead on each wire.

2 Using the wire cutters, cut either four, five, or six pieces of wire into 7½-inch lengths. With the pliers, make a tiny loop at one end of each wire.

3 Carefully take one strand of beads from the bunch, and tape one end to your work surface (see A, above left). Pulling strand taut, transfer strung beads to the wire by feeding the wire through the holes (see B, above left). Slide the beads down the wire toward the loop; leave just enough room to loop the open end of the wire, preventing beads from slipping off. The beads should be slightly loose on the wire.

4 Once all the wires are beaded, shape them into a candy cane by holding the wires together at one end and twisting them together (see photograph, left); keep the beaded wires even and the surface smooth. Bend wires at the top into the gentle hook of a cane. Some ends will be uneven; you can adjust them by removing a few beads where necessary and making those wires shorter.

choosing beads

Beads come in a variety of styles. Look closely, and you'll discover that each strain of bead has a distinct shape and sparkle. Rocailles are small glass beads with a square hole lined in silver. Tri-cut beads are tiny and faceted and have a round hole. Fire-polished crystal beads are faceted and can be large or small. And druks are smooth, perfect spheres. The smallest beads usually appear as spacers in beaded jewelry and ornaments, but they can be used to great effect by themselves if a sufficient number are brought together. All of these styles are usually sold on "strands," which often come in "hanks" of 10 to 12 strands.

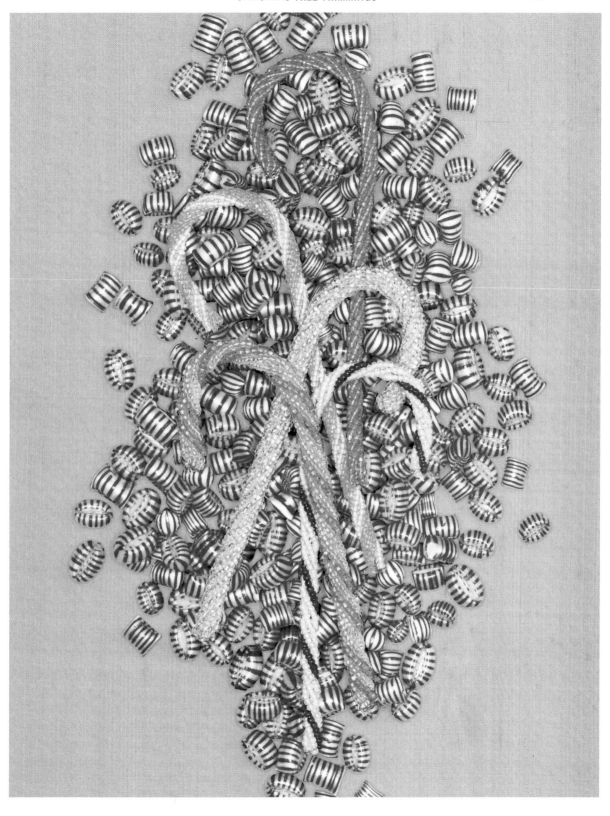

glittered paper ornaments

A Christmas tree dusted with "snow" looks even frostier when decorated exclusively in shades of silver, white, and cream. Pretty paper-and-glitter ornaments, inspired by classic German decorations, are simple and fun to make and mix well with vintage metallic pieces. When working with glitter, especially ground-glass varieties, wear gloves and a dust mask to protect yourself from fine particles.

WHAT YOU WILL NEED Glittered paper ornament templates (see page 359), card stock, small scissors or craft knife, small paintbrush, white craft glue, glitter, fine paintbrush or applicator bottle and tip, thin ribbons, hot-glue gun, hole punch, silver twine, beads

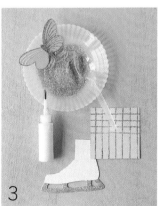

1 Download and print templates onto white or off-white card stock; then use small scissors or a craft knife to cut out shapes.

2 For one-color ornaments, such as the dove, use a small paintbrush to apply glue to one side. Sprinkle with glitter, working over a bowl; shake off excess. Let dry; repeat on opposite side to keep paper from warping.

3 For multiple colors or details, such as on the ice skate, create designs using glue in a bottle with a fine-tip applicator; then sprinkle on glitter, and shake off excess. (Work on one small section at a time so glue doesn't dry before glitter is applied.) Apply other colors of glitter after each section dries.

4 To attach thin ribbon and bows to gift ornament, squeeze a line of glue over glitter; press ribbon into place, tucking cut ends under. To attach butterfly to scalloped background, apply hot glue to body; leave wings free. Bend wings upward once glue has dried. Punch a hole at top of each ornament, as indicated on template, thread with silver twine, add a bead, and tie to make a loop for hanging.

china-inspired ornaments

With a nod to centuries-old ceramic arts, these ornaments look to popular styles of china: caneware (unglazed yellow stoneware), Old Paris porcelain (white bone china), and drabware (earthenware characterized by its olive- to coffee-toned glaze and gilded details). We crafted the ornaments using Paperclay modeling material and wooden springerle molds, traditionally used to make anise-flavored holiday cookies.

WHAT YOU WILL NEED Acrylic paint (2 tablespoons yellow and ½ tablespoon brown for caneware; 2 tablespoons green and ½ tablespoon brown for drabware), small bowl, gloves, spoon, Paperclay (1 pound blocks), nonstick baking mat, mold release (available at art-supply stores; follow manufacturer's instructions), springerle molds (available online), cookie cutter, dough scraper, wire racks, fine sandpaper, water-based size adhesive, thin paintbrush, gilding leaf, dry paintbrush, pencil, patterned paper (for backing), scissors, small brush, white craft glue, grosgrain ribbon (¼- to ⅜-inch wide for small and medium ornaments, ⅜-inch wide for larger ones)

1 If making caneware or drabware ornaments, mix paint in a bowl. Wearing gloves, spoon mixture onto 1 pound block of clay. Gently knead until color is uniform throughout. (If making Old Paris porcelain-inspired ornaments, do not add paint to clay.)

2 Working on a nonstick baking mat, coat springerle mold with mold release. Press clay into mold, spreading it beyond the edges. Flip mold over, and push on the back until the clay is an even thickness: for small- and medium-size ornaments, ¼ to ⅜ inch thick; for larger ornaments, about ⅜ inch thick (if made too thin, the ornaments will buckle as they dry). Carefully peel away clay. Cut excess from edges using cookie cutter or dough scraper. Smooth edges with your fingers. Lay ornaments on a rack overnight or until they are completely dry. If ornaments warp while drying, bend them back into shape. Once dry, sand rough edges.

3 Before gilding, make sure ornaments are dry (moisture can cause the leaf to tarnish). Use a thin paintbrush to apply size to the relief. Let size set until it becomes tacky, about 20 minutes. Wearing gloves, gently pick up a piece of gilding leaf and lightly place it over the size. Use a clean, dry paintbrush to brush the leaf into the details or on the flat surface. Lightly buff the remaining leaf off and smooth the gilded area with a gloved finger.

4 Trace ornament onto patterned paper, wrong side up; cut out. Cut a 2-inch length of ribbon. Loop and glue it to the top of the ornament back. Brush glue onto back of ornament, and affix paper. Cut a length of ribbon long enough to wrap around the outer edge of the ornament. Glue ribbon, starting and ending at top, so seam is in line with top loop.

tree-trimming techniques

Your tree should act as a stage for your ornaments. Look for one with broad, sweeping layers, and then prune it to exaggerate that. Spruces, in particular blues and Norways, have natural tiers. The goal in pruning a tree is to gently mimic the form of an artificial feather tree, which has plenty of space between branches for decorations to hang freely.

glossary of tools

1 CLUMP MOSS Use this greenery (available at online florist-supply shops) to hide pebbles and tree-stand hardware.

2 FELT Place a square of this soft fabric under the container to prevent scratches and facilitate moving the tree.

3 PLASTIC SHEETING Line the container with this material to avoid leaks.

4 WORK GLOVES Don a pair of these to protect hands when transporting the tree indoors and during the pruning.

5 PEBBLES Pour around the trunk to stabilize the tree stand. Pebbles will also help retain moisture, so you won't need to water the tree as frequently.

6 FLORAL SHEARS This gardening tool is perfect for pruning thin branches.

7 RUBBER GLOVES Wear these while you string the lights to protect your hands from prickly needles, which can be especially irritating with spruce trees.

8 TREE STAND This device is what holds the tree upright. To prevent toppling, look for one with a wide, flat base, such as this bucket version. It should be able to accommodate at least one gallon of water. Take measurements to ensure the stand will fit inside your decorative container.

9 HAND DRILL (shown in tree stand) Use this to make a small hole in the center of the trunk base so that the tree will take in more water.

10 HANDSAW Help the tree absorb water by cutting about an inch off the trunk before putting it in the stand. A saw is also good for removing very thick branches.

11 GARDEN LOPPERS This is the tool of choice for trimming thick branches.

the basics

There's no right or wrong way to decorate a tree, but if you want to emulate the style of our crafts editors, heed the following guidelines.

POTTING

These 5 steps will help you to achieve a safe, stable, and stylish tree.

1 Lay felt (A) underneath the container to protect the floor.

2 Stack bricks inside planter (B) to raise the tree if necessary.

3 Place the tree stand (C) inside the planter, followed by the tree.

4 Pour pebbles (D) into the stand for added stability.

5 Finish off by adding clump moss (E).

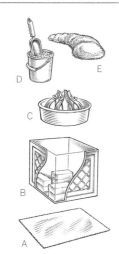

PRUNING

Norway and blue spruces are naturally symmetrical, but their branches have awkward growths that keep ornaments from hanging freely. Clean them up with a little judicious pruning.

1 Stand the tree upright, and study it from a distance to see which areas need pruning.

2 Prune the small growths that jut straight out from the top and bottom of the branches. The lighter sections depicted in the illustration above represent the ones you'd want to trim away.

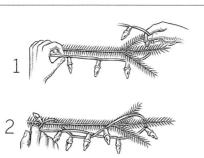

LIGHTING

This technique will play up the depth of the tree better than simply draping lights only around the perimeter, while also concealing the wires.

1 Starting at a bottom bough, string lights along underside of each branch. When you get near the end, loop the lights around the top of the branch.

2 Work back to the tree trunk, winding around the branch and light strand. Continue around the tree. Reverse the procedure on upper branches (or those above the eye level of an average adult), stringing lights first along the top, then back around the bottom.

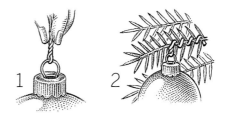

HANGING

Suspend ornaments from tinned copper wire instead of manufactured hooks, which can slip off branches, causing breakage.

1 Thread a 5-inch piece of wire through the ornament loop; twist the wire around itself several times to secure.

2 To hang, wrap the other end of the wire around the branch until the ornament is secure.

DECK
THE HALLS

calling-bird stockings

Though silent, our four calling birds still herald the bounty within the stockings they grace. The stockings are made from luxurious mohair, wool, and cashmere. Carefully stored, they will last for many holiday seasons. On the mantel, pepper-berries spill from pots and holly branches grace a creamy white pitcher.

WHAT YOU WILL NEED Calling-bird stocking templates (see page 359), pencil, woven fabric (such as wool, mohair, or cashmere), scissors, straight pins, sewing machine, iron, large and small bird templates (see page 359), wool felt, white craft glue, feathers, small paintbrush, sequins or beads, needle and thread

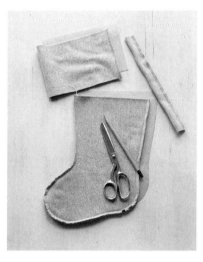

1 Download and print the stocking templates. Trace onto fabric. Cut one body, cuff, and hanging loop from fabric. Flip template over, and cut out second body and cuff for other side of stocking. Pin stocking pieces together, right sides facing; sew along perimeter, with a ¼-inch seam allowance. Leave top open. Carefully notch along curves, as shown, so stocking will lie flat when turned right-side out. Pin two cuff pieces together, right sides facing; sew along short edges. Fold hanging loop in half lengthwise; sew up long side.

2 Turn body right-side out. To attach cuff, tuck it, wrong-side out, inside top of stocking so edges are flush and seam lines up with back seam of stocking. Sew along top edge; turn cuff upward as shown. Steam the open seam. Roll cuff down so that it covers seam between cuff and body. Fold loose edge of cuff under; stitch hem. Turn hanging loop right-side out; sew it inside cuff at desired length.

3 Download and print the large and small bird templates. Cut out templates and trace onto wool felt. Cut body and wings out of the felt. Glue each wing to the body (with the upraised wing on the back and the down-turned wing on the front). To adorn the wings and tail with feathers, strip the down from each feather, and glue the feather to the felt using the small paintbrush. Attach a sequin or bead to make an eye. Tack bird to a stocking with a couple of hand-stitches through its upraised wing.

paper evergreens

Paper trees made from circles in graduated sizes are as pretty as origami versions but much easier to make. Wooden spools serve as tree stands; pretty white plates covered with faux "snow" double as containers. A few glass cloches (bell-shaped domes) and mercury-glass votives complete the display.

WHAT YOU WILL NEED Adjustable circle cutter, cutting mat, green card stock, bone folder, craft knife, 12-inch wooden skewers, hot-glue gun, wooden spools, gold beads

1 For large Christmas trees, use an adjustable circle cutter to make 2-, 3-, 4-, 5-, and 6-inch-diameter circles from card stock (for small trees, omit the 6-inch circle).

2 Fold each circle in half 4 times with the bone folder (above, left). While circles are folded, snip off the tip of each piece, forming a very small hole in the center.

3 Place the smallest circle on the pointed end of a wooden skewer, letting the tip poke through the hole in the circle. With a hot-glue gun, dab underside of circle, where paper and skewer meet. Hold for 10 seconds to secure.

4 Working one at a time from smallest circle to largest, slide remaining circles onto skewer; secure with glue (above, right).

5 Insert bottom of skewer into a spool; remove, and cut skewer to desired height (we cut ours to 6, 9, and 10 inches), keeping in mind that only the spool should be visible beneath standing tree. Return skewer to spool; secure with glue. Add a dot of glue to the top of the skewer, and attach a gold bead.

golden walnut ball

A twist on the traditional ball of mistletoe, this large hanging ornament is studded with gold-painted walnuts and crowned with boughs of bay. Monofilament is used to support the ball as it hangs; the wide satin ribbon is strictly decorative.

WHAT YOU WILL NEED 3¾-inch screw eye, 8-inch Styrofoam ball, floral spray (in brilliant gold), walnuts, hot-glue gun, monofilament, wire, wide satin ribbon, bay boughs

1 Insert the screw eye into the Styrofoam ball. Working in a well-ventilated area and over a protected work surface, coat ball with gold floral spray.

2 Affix walnuts using a low-melt glue gun and coat nuts with floral spray; because it is thinner than traditional spray paint, you will need to spray the walnuts twice to cover them thoroughly. Be sure to allow the first coat to dry completely before applying the second (the paint dries quickly).

3 Hang up the ball with a length of monofilament attached to the screw eye. Wire a wide bow and ribbon to screw eye (see page 342 for instructions on tying a classic bow). Secure several bay boughs to top of ball with hot glue.

ribbon card holders

Displaying the cards you receive each year is a lovely holiday tradition, especially when you create a set of keepsake card holders. Here, ribbon card holders descend from extra-large tuxedo bows, bound tightly in the middle for a billowing effect; cards slide into "pockets" created by gluing narrow satin ribbon at various intervals.

WHAT YOU WILL NEED Scissors, 4-inch-wide ribbon (about 70 inches long), card envelopes, 9-mm-wide ribbon (about 50 inches long), fabric glue, 20-gauge wire, removable adhesive hooks (for hanging)

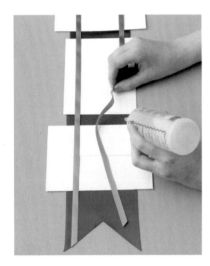  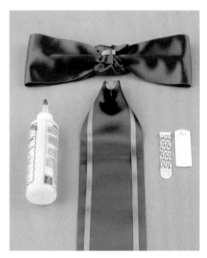

1 Cut a 40-inch (or longer) length of wide ribbon. To make an even notch in the bottom, fold ribbon in half lengthwise and cut on an angle from outer edge to fold; unfold. Since you'll likely be making this before holiday cards arrive, lay out 5 or 6 card envelopes along the front of the ribbon, some horizontally and others vertically, keeping a ½-inch space between them. Lay a narrow ribbon down each side (about ½ inch in from the edge); trim ends to match angle of notch. With envelopes as your guide, glue the narrow ribbons to the wide ribbon between envelopes. Slide envelopes out.

2 With a 25-inch-long wide ribbon, make a 12-inch tuxedo bow: Fold ends of a piece of ribbon in toward the center, overlapping them; secure with fabric glue. Flatten at center and glue to secure. Cover center with a second piece of ribbon, gluing at back of bow. Wrap center tightly to cinch bow. At back, knot narrow ribbon around center band, then rotate narrow ribbon so its knot is concealed inside. This will be the loop from which bow will hang.

3 Cinch top of tail: Twist a piece of wire into a loop. Fold the top corners of ribbon under about 1 inch (top edges should be flush); at the same time, press the top center in with your thumbs, forming the shape shown. Secure the ribbon with dabs of fabric glue, and glue wire to center. Using a removable adhesive hook, hang tail first, and then bow.

teacup topiaries

Coordinating with a wall display of pink lusterware plates, miniature topiaries of Alberta spruce, boxwood, and juniper rest in pink lusterware teacups on the mantel; tiny tree toppers are made of glass beads threaded onto straight pins. To make uniform trees, start with pieces of evergreen that are exactly the same length.

WHAT YOU WILL NEED Floral-foam cone (4-by-9-inch or 5-by-12-inch), Surform shaver (available at hardware stores), teacups, evergreen pieces (Alberta spruce, boxwood, and juniper), straight pins, wire cutters, 28-gauge wire, pearl-topped pins, glass beads

1 Trim the bottom of a floral-foam cone so it fits inside a teacup. If the sides of the cone need to be trimmed, use the Surform shaver. Soak the foam cone in water for 30 minutes.

2 While the cone soaks, cut 1-inch pieces of evergreen; trim the greenery from the bottom half of each piece.

3 Nestle the cone in a teacup. Starting from the bottom and working in rows, insert pieces of evergreen into the foam.

4 For a tree topper: Cut off the top of a straight pin with wire cutters, and wire it to a pearl-topped pin to extend its length. Slide glass beads onto pin; we used a large bead between two smaller ones. Insert the wired pin into the top of the cone.

A FESTIVE TABLE

candy basket centerpiece

In Germany, a red-and-white mushroom, or "praktische pilzkunde," is an auspicious token and a popular holiday tree motif. Ours sprout from dried moss atop round containers set in the center of the table. These, along with some pouch-filled baskets nestled in faux snow, hold candies for dinner guests to take home as favors.

WHAT YOU WILL NEED Styrofoam balls (1 to 2½ inches), white craft glue, cotton quilt batting (dyed red, according to dye manufacturer's instructions), fabric dye, flat paintbrush, straight pins, white cotton pipe cleaners, scissors, clear glass-shard glitter, round wooden boxes, pencil, illustration board, pinking shears, icicle template (see page 359), paintbrush, white acrylic paint, clear fine glass glitter, hot-glue gun, dried moss (available at crafts stores), kraft paper, spray adhesive, round cardboard boxes, red crepe paper, screw punch, silver cord, double-sided tape, wrapped candy

1 Make the mushrooms: Cut Styrofoam ball in half (for cap); press in flat side to make it concave. Mix 2 parts craft glue and 1 part water. Tear a few small pieces of dyed cotton batting; press around the curved top and stretch to cover bottom. Using a flat paintbrush, saturate batting with glue mixture, pressing onto foam. Repeat to make more mushroom tops. Let dry 1 hour. Repeat process to apply a second layer of red batting. Using a pin, make a hole in bottom; insert a pipe cleaner (for stem), and trim. Brush cap with glue; sprinkle with clear glass-shard glitter.

2 Make moss containers: Trace wooden box lid on illustration board; cut out with pinking shears (for base). Download and print the icicle template; trace onto illustration board. Cut out; trim to fit lid. Paint box, lid, base, and icicles with white acrylic paint; let dry. Glue icicles and base to box. Paint icicles and box with craft glue (avoid lid overhangs); sprinkle with clear fine-glass glitter. Hot-glue dried moss to lid. Wrap box with kraft paper to protect it; coat moss with spray adhesive, and sprinkle with clear glass-shard glitter. Push mushrooms into moss.

3 Make candy baskets: Trace round cardboard box lid on illustration board. Cut out with pinking shears (for base). Cut a handle. Reduce icicle template; trace onto illustration board. Cut out; trim to fit basket. Paint all parts with white acrylic; let dry. Glue parts together; apply glue and fine-glass glitter. Cut a piece of crepe paper to fit around circumference of basket and extend over top edge (forming a column that will go in basket). Punch holes down its length, ½ inch in from a long edge; thread silver cord through. Secure in basket with double-sided tape. Fill with candy; tie.

gilded pears

A wicker basket filled with gold-dusted pears looks straight out of a fairy tale. The arrangement is filled out with magnolia leaves that are also transformed with gold (in the form of floral paint), sprigs of fresh cedar, and a gorgeous green satin ribbon. Each guest is welcomed to the table with a beribboned, gold-dusted pear.

WHAT YOU WILL NEED Nontoxic gold petal dust, pears, small new paintbrush, small bowl, basket, magnolia leaves, floral spray (in brilliant gold), cedar sprigs, wide satin ribbon

FOR GOLD-DUSTED PEARS Wash pears and dry completely. Handle the fruit by the stem. Place petal dust in the bowl; apply to fruit with a paintbrush, touching up as necessary.

FOR GOLD MAGNOLIA LEAVES Working in a well-ventilated area, coat shiny side of magnolia leaves with gold floral spray; let dry.

FOR ARRANGEMENT Place the gold pears in the basket; touch up with gold petal dust. Tuck gold-sprayed magnolia leaves among the fruit and cedar sprigs around basket edge. Tie ribbons on each end of the handles.

petal dust

Bakers use petal dust (also known as luster dust) to give natural shadings and a dewy glow to gum-paste flowers and fruit used to adorn wedding and other festive cakes. It also adds a wonderful shimmer to fresh fruit. Using nontoxic petal dust, available at baking supply stores, on the fresh pears will ensure they are still safe to eat.

carnation clusters

Cloaked in carnations in shades of red and white, floral foam balls beautifully brighten an entryway or table for a holiday party. The intense colors and striped varieties, along with luminous glass ornaments and footed glass vessels, transform these supermarket staples into an unexpectedly opulent display.

WHAT YOU WILL NEED 5 dozen carnations (in red or red and white), scissors, 4½-inch floral-foam ball, glass vessel, small wired glass ball ornaments (optional)

Before creating the clusters, condition the flowers to strengthen and open the blooms: Cut the stems at an angle above or below (but not on) a swollen node, and submerge them in clean water for at least 12 hours before using. After the flowers have been conditioned, immerse the floral-foam ball in water for 20 minutes; let drain. Cut the stems at an angle, 2 to 3 inches from heads. Place ball on top of a glass vessel; working in rows from top to bottom, push stems into foam, clustering blooms together and spacing evenly. To cover the bottom of the ball, hold it in your hand and fill in the remaining open space with more flowers. Push in wired glass ornaments between blooms if desired.

silver and red table setting

Bouquets of bold-red amaryllis tied with stiff silver ribbon looks stunning displayed down the center of a hushed gray, white, and silver table setting. The handcrafted napkin rings and the beading detail on the rims of the Nymphenburg porcelain plates seem as delicate as a spray of frozen raindrops. To make the napkin rings, simply thread silver mesh beads onto silver string, and tie. Finish by tying on a bow of light-gray ribbon.

embellished evergreen wreath

Evergreen wreaths represent the best of holiday decorating. But if fashioning one from scratch won't fit on your to-do list, here is an easy way to add beauty and polish to an unadorned premade wreath. To create the glittering example shown opposite, a noble fir wreath was trimmed with silvery ornaments (we used approximately 100 ornaments of varying sizes) and sprigs of seeded eucalyptus. For vintage appeal, the ornaments were "antiqued" to resemble the collection of mercury-glass vessels displayed on the mantel below (see opposite).

WHAT YOU WILL NEED Gouache (in white and black), small bowls, 2 sponges, wired silver-ball ornaments (we used 2-inch, 1¼-inch, 1-inch, ¾-inch, and ½-inch sizes), tissues, wired floral picks, seeded eucalyptus sprigs, 24-inch-diameter noble fir wreath

ANTIQUING GLASS ORNAMENTS

1 Place 1 teaspoon each of white and black gouache paint in separate bowls. Dilute with water, a few drops at a time, until paint has the consistency of heavy cream.

2 Working with one ornament at a time, dab entire surface with sponge dipped in white gouache mixture. While ornament is still wet, use tissues to gently dab ornament, creating a mottled look (above, left).

3 Using another sponge, lightly and sparingly dab the ornament in a few places with black gouache. Use clean tissues to lighten and blur the black spots, creating the appearance of flaked mercury glass. Let dry at least 1 hour.

MAKING THE WREATH

1 Align each ornament's wire with one floral pick. Wrap pick wire around both to secure (above, center). Attach each eucalyptus sprig to a pick, using the same process (above, right).

2 Insert largest ornaments at the top of the wreath. Add other ornaments, varying sizes and positions as desired, using smaller ornaments along the wreath's outer edges; reserve the tiniest ornaments to dot around wreath bottom once other ornaments are inserted.

3 Insert eucalyptus sprigs around ornaments, using leafier stems and fuller bud sprigs at the wreath's top, and tapering fullness of additions as you work down wreath sides.

4 Add tiniest ornaments and a few remaining individual eucalyptus leaves wired to picks to bottom of wreath.

ribbon-poinsettia wreath

*It's remarkable how ribbons weave their way into so many aspects of the holidays.
Stock up on lustrous lengths of satin, velvet, and other cloth ribbons. They are
more versatile than you might imagine (and they're also reusable—don't forget
to save the beautiful ones that come your way). Wide ribbon strips can be cinched
at their middles and wired to form poinsettia "flowers," complete with center "pips."
Pinned to a Styrofoam form, the ribbon poinsettias make an exquisite keepsake
wreath. Hang with a length of the same wide ribbon used to make the flowers.*

WHAT YOU WILL NEED Red ribbon (2½ to 4 inches wide, for flowers), straight pins, fabric-covered wire, "pips" (artificial stamens; available at crafts stores) or beads, white craft glue, green ribbon (2 to 3 inches wide, for leaves), Styrofoam wreath form, Surform shaver

1 To make ribbon poinsettia, cut a 10-inch length of red ribbon. Cut it diagonally into 3 diamonds. Pinch each diamond across its short axis, to pleat; pin. Form a 6-petaled blossom with the 3 diamonds. Secure with wire around centers, twisting in back; remove pins. Remove stems from "pips" and glue to front of blossom (you can use beads instead), or glue on stamens after poinsettias are attached to wreath.

2 Add leaves: Cut 5-inch lengths of green ribbon. With right side down, fold ribbon into sideways L shape. Make crease at middle of first fold as you bring upper leg of "L" to cover lower leg; edges will line up in a house shape. Pleat open end of house-shaped ribbon with your fingers; pin in place.

3 Shave edges of the Styrofoam form with a Surform shaver, making them rounder. Wrap with ribbon; pin ends to secure. Attach poinsettias and leaves with straight pins, hiding pins within ribbon folds and overlapping blossoms as you go until wreath form is completely covered.

paper-doily wreath

A delicate-looking wreath creates the magical effect of candles flickering in the snow, yet is surprisingly sturdy—and easy to put together. Wire wreath forms are strung with twinkling lights that are nestled in frilly, doily-like paper bouquet holders known as "Biedermeiermanschetten."

WHAT YOU WILL NEED 24-inch wire wreath form, 30-inch wire wreath form, 24-gauge wire, wire cutters, white spray paint, white holiday lights (20-foot strand), scissors, paper bouquet holders (available online; we used ten 8.8-inch, twenty 4.8-inch, and fifty 3.2-inch sizes)

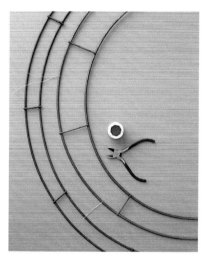

1 Working on a covered surface in a well-ventilated area, lay the 24-inch wire wreath form inside the 30-inch one. Attach them with 24-gauge wire at 6 to 8 evenly spaced points (above left). Coat combined wreath form with white spray paint. Let dry.

2 Wrap the wreath form with the strand of holiday lights (test lights beforehand), leaving the plug end unwrapped (as much as is needed to plug into socket).

3 With scissors, widen the center-hole slits slightly in the paper bouquet holders, then poke a finger through each hole (from front to back) to create openings large enough to accommodate a lightbulb.

4 Beginning with largest ones, place bouquet holders evenly around wreath, slipping a light through each hole so that bulb bases, not bulbs, rest against paper. (From time to time, hang wreath, and step back to ensure that the arrangement is balanced and attractive.)

5 Add remaining bouquet holders in descending size order. Use smallest bouquet holders to cover centers of larger ones and to fill in any gaps. Hang wreath near an outlet; unplug when unattended.

SEASON'S GREETINGS

yarn cards

The winter holidays offer plenty of time-honored symbols to play with: snowmen, wreaths, fir trees, snowflakes, mittens, candy canes, and more. Experiment with yarn in different colors, weights, and textures—even on the same card—to create simple, cheerful outlines. An ornament design requires only a couple of curves, while several graduated lengths of yarn render a minimalist tree.

WHAT YOU WILL NEED Pencil, scratch paper, card stock or blank cards, white craft glue, applicator bottle and tip (or round-headed pin), yarn, small scissors

1 The trick to creating a clean design is to include only the details necessary to make the image recognizable. Practice on scratch paper until you have a satisfactory design to work with. Lightly pencil a clean version of your sketch onto a blank card or piece of card stock.

2 Trace the drawing with craft glue in a bottle with a fine-tip applicator (or apply with a round-headed pin).

3 Carefully place yarn on the glue. Let dry completely before trimming away excess yarn with small scissors.

quilled christmas cards

The art of quilling lends itself well to seasonal shapes such as snowflakes, evergreen trees, and candy canes. Strips of paper are shaped by bending and curling the ends around a tool, as you would a ribbon. The finished products should be hand-delivered rather than sent through the mail, to prevent crushing.

WHAT YOU WILL NEED Quilling paper, paper trimmer, card stock or blank cards, slotted quilling tool (available online), small sharp scissors, pencil, white craft glue, applicator bottle and tip, fine-pointed tweezers

Use a paper trimmer to cut quilling paper into strips of desired widths (or use precut strips). Make scrolls (see page 343 for quilling instructions and a glossary of scroll shapes): To make a tree, form several V-shaped scrolls in different sizes. For a snowflake, make V-shaped scrolls, heart-shaped scrolls, marquise scrolls, and tight circles. For a candy cane, form 6 red tight circles and 5 white tight circles; cut out paper leaves. Sketch the design very lightly on a card with a pencil. Glue along pencil marks, one section at a time. Use tweezers to place quilled scrolls, on edge, over the glue; hold in place for 15 seconds to allow glue to set. Glue remaining scrolls in place to complete the design.

giftlike greetings

Here's a great project for presenting gift cards or certificates, cash, and other flat items. Use scraps of ribbon of various widths and colors to tie tiny bows onto the front of a card; secure the ribbon inside the card with double-sided tape, and glue a sheet of paper on top to cover. To mimic the blue and green cards, top bands of ribbon with a bow; the latter has one less band of ribbon and a knot-style bow. To craft a card similar to the hot pink one, make two horizontal bands of red ribbon, and two vertical; tie red bows where the ribbons intersect. To make a three-ribbon card like the red-patterned one, attach three strips of thin silver ribbon, and attach three bows, each at a different height.

pop-up cards

A handmade pop-up card is always unique and anything but two-dimensional. And as impressive as a pop-up looks, it's deceptively easy to make. With a few basic techniques you can create a wide range of shapes, colors, and decorative details. The snowman and snowflake pop-ups are decorated with glitter and glue, and inscribed with a red pen. You can use almost any type of paper or card stock to make these cards; just be sure it's sturdy enough to withstand cutting and folding.

WHAT YOU WILL NEED Heavyweight paper or card stock, pop-up card templates (see page 359), pencil, craft knife, paintbrush, white craft glue, glitter, bowl

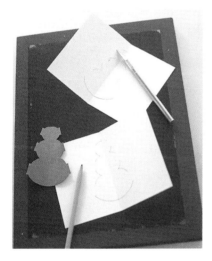 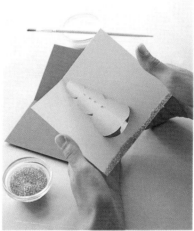

1 The cards are composed of an inner card glued to a stiffer backing that provides support and hides any slits or tabs made to attach figures. It's easier to fold the backing before the interior of the card has been glued on. Download, print, and cut out the templates. Trace onto folded card stock, centering the image over the fold. Cut along shape with a craft knife, leaving it attached at the tabs.

2 Push the shape forward from behind while slightly closing the card to crease the shape down the middle. Using the paintbrush, apply glue to areas you want to decorate with glitter. Sprinkle with glitter; working over a bowl, shake off excess. Let dry completely before gluing card into the larger prefolded backing.

GIVE CHEER

rickrack gift bags

Make a bunch of simple felt sacks to present small gifts for Christmas, and adorn them with rickrack designs. Each sack has side seams; the bottom corners are folded toward the center and tacked. Handles are made from nothing more than two lengths of intertwined trim. Embellish the front of the bag with a contrasting ornament. See pages 275 and 279 for a variety of rickrack designs and how-to instructions.

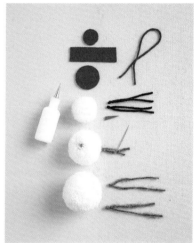

pom-pom snowman

Made of white pom-poms, felt, and ribbon, this frosty friend never has to melt.
He makes a great toy for a child; add a loop to the hat, and he becomes an ornament.

WHAT YOU WILL NEED Pom-pom maker, yarn (gray, black, and red), yarn needle, felt (orange and red), white craft glue, invisible thread, twill tape

Make two 2¼-inch pom-poms and one 1¾-inch pom-pom (see page 342 for instructions; or use store-bought pom-poms). Trim one large pom-pom to be slightly smaller. Cut 3 pieces of gray yarn (for buttons) and 2 of black yarn (for eyes), each 5¼ inches long; knot each in center. Thread ends of each yarn piece through pom-poms (use a yarn needle, and work with one end at a time) where shown (above right), tying yarn in back. Glue on orange felt carrot nose. For hat, cut ¾- and 1¼-inch circles and a 2¼-by-¾-inch rectangle of red felt. Sew a yarn loop to small circle if you are making an ornament. Glue rectangle into a cylinder and to the edge of small circle; glue to large circle. Sew up from the bottoms with needle and thread, sewing through centers of pom-poms to join them and sewing through bottom of hat; then sew back down through centers, and knot. Tie on a tiny twill-tape scarf.

winter wonderland snow globes

The shimmering magic of snowfall is always transfixing, whether it's outside the window or inside a classic toy. Making snow globes yourself lets you create wintery scenes straight out of your own imagination. Look for plastic or ceramic figurines (metal ones are prone to rust) at flea markets, hobby or model-railroad shops, and online. This is an especially fun project to do with children; the globes make great gifts for teachers and classmates.

WHAT YOU WILL NEED Glass jars with lids, oil-based enamel paint and paintbrush (optional), sandpaper, plastic or ceramic figurines and/or synthetic evergreen tips (available at florist-supply shops), silicone glue, distilled water, clear glitter, glycerin (available at drugstores)

1 Paint the jar lids with oil-based enamel paint, if desired (work in a well-ventilated area on a protected surface). Let dry. Sand the inside of the lid until the surface is rough, so glue will adhere to it.

2 Arrange figurines and/or synthetic evergreen tips on the inside of the lid. Glue in place, and let dry completely.

3 Fill the jar almost to the top with distilled water. Do not be tempted to use tap water instead of distilled, as it can turn yellow over time. (Boiling tap water does not remove impurities, either.) Add a pinch of glitter and a few drops of glycerin. Apply a ring of glue to the mouth of the jar. Screw on the lid tightly, being careful not to dislodge the figurines.

about glycerin

Adding a dash of glycerin—a clear compound used in soap-making—to the water in a snow globe will keep the glitter from falling too quickly. Don't add too much, though, or the glitter will stick to the bottom of the jar when it's flipped.

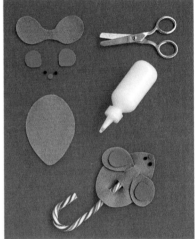

candy cane mice

Two Christmas icons—mice and candy canes—are combined in these delightful felt creatures. With their red-and-white-striped tails and cheerful felt details, they make great gifts for—and especially from—children. Spend an afternoon crafting them for friends and relatives, or give them out as holiday party favors.

WHAT YOU WILL NEED Candy cane mouse template (see page 359), pencil, felt (we used wool in a variety of colors), scissors, white craft glue, candy canes

Download and print the mouse template. With a pencil, trace ears and body onto felt; cut out. Cut inner ears and a dot for a nose from contrasting-color felt; cut dots for eyes from black felt. Glue the face and inner ears in place; let dry completely. Make slits in body for ears and tail where marked by dotted lines (to make cutting easier, fold felt across center of slits, and snip). Slip ears through slits at front; then slide wrapped candy cane through body slits, tucking end between the ear piece and the body on the underside.

snowman-topped pencils

Put these gifts together assembly-line style, and you'll have one for every kid in the class. You can also give one with a blank notebook; attach the two with red-and-white baker's twine.

WHAT YOU WILL NEED 1-inch Styrofoam balls, pencils, white craft glue, paintbrush, clear glitter, spoon, small bowl, orange felt, black seed beads, narrow ribbon

Make one of two 1-inch Styrofoam balls a bit smaller by pressing uniformly against a flat surface. Push pencil eraser into bigger ball by ¼ inch; remove, coat eraser with glue; reinsert. Glue on smaller ball for head. Brush the snowman with glue; working over a bowl, spoon on glitter; tap off the excess. Let dry. Glue on a tiny piece of orange felt for a nose and black seed beads for eyes. Let dry 30 minutes. Tie on a small piece of ribbon for a scarf.

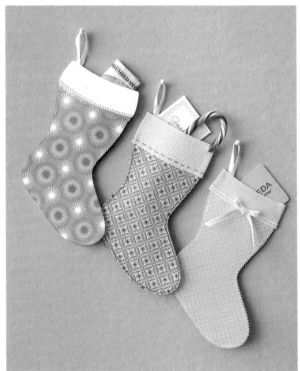

money and gift card wrappers

As gifts, currency and gift cards are often the perfect fit for a host of people on your list, but finding a way to package them creatively can be a challenge. Overcome the unsentimental nature of such gifts (and enhance the element of surprise) with clever, handcrafted wrappers that disguise their telltale shapes.

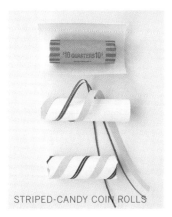

STRIPED-CANDY COIN ROLLS

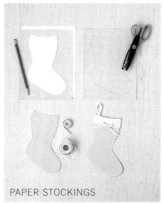

PAPER STOCKINGS

RIBBON POCKETS
AND POUCHES

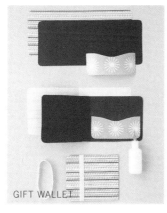

GIFT WALLET

STRIPED-CANDY COIN ROLLS Wrap a roll of coins in plain paper. Add decorative stripes by attaching colored quilling strips with double-sided tape; wind tightly around roll in a spiral motion, and tape ends. Wrap in cellophane, twist ends, and attach tags with yarn.

PAPER STOCKINGS Download and print stocking template (see page 359). Cut out; trace onto patterned paper. Place a second sheet under first, wrong sides facing; sew together, just inside lines. Cut out, leaving a small border. Decorate tops with paper or ribbon, securing with double-sided tape. Glue a tiny ribbon loop inside.

RIBBON POCKETS AND POUCHES For the pockets, buy precut tags with grommets. Cut a 3½-inch length of wide ribbon. Fold each cut end under by ¼ inch; glue. Sew bottom and side edges to tag to form pocket. For the pouches, fold a 14-inch-long piece of wide ribbon in half, wrong sides facing. Iron along fold, pin. Sew up long sides. Remove pins. Trim edges of open end with scalloping scissors. Slip gift inside. Cinch and knot a bit of ribbon or twine to secure.

GIFT WALLET Lay open a real wallet; trace around onto two pieces of card stock; cut out. Glue pieces back to back. For pocket, trace closed wallet onto wrapping paper. Cut out, and trim off top half. Glue to paper billfold at edges. Topstitch around billfold and side and bottom of pocket with a sewing machine, leaving ½-inch seam allowance. Wrap elastic ribbon snugly around billfold to overlap; cut, and staple into a band.

holly block-printed linens

A bright trail of hand-printed holly branches transforms plain white table linens into festive gifts. The leaves are made with a custom-carved block, and the berries (which also appear in clusters on the cocktail napkins) are created using a pencil eraser.

WHAT YOU WILL NEED Holly block-printed linens template (see page 359), scissors, tracing paper, pencil, soft-carve block (available at crafts stores and online), tape, bone folder, linoleum cutter, paintbrush, fabric paint, linens (dinner and cocktail napkins, tablecloths, table runner), spoon, pencil with unused eraser, fabric ink pad

1 Download and print template, enlarging or reducing it to desired size, and cut out. Lay a sheet of tracing paper over the template. Trace the design with a pencil. Shade the areas you'll carve out. Arrange a soft-carve block on a flat surface, and position tracing paper, design-side down, on top of it. Secure the paper to the block with tape. Use the bone folder to rub the entire surface of the tracing paper against the block; this will transfer the design to the linoleum block. Remove the paper and tape. Holding the linoleum cutter with the hollow side of the blade facing up, carve the marked areas. Use your other hand as a guide, keeping it clear of the blade's path. Working slowly, begin with shallow cuts; if you dig the cutter down into the block, it could cut all the way through.

2 With the paintbrush, apply fabric paint to coat the uncarved surface of the block. Place the fabric facedown over the paint-coated block. Lightly rub the back of the fabric with the back of a spoon, then gently pull away. To make holly berries, press the tip of the pencil eraser into the fabric ink pad, then stamp over holly leaves. Set paint and ink according to manufacturer's instructions.

TAGS, TIES, AND TOPPERS

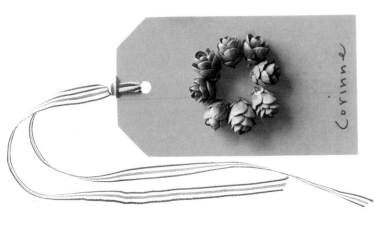

embellished tags

Add extra charm to your holiday packaging with a little help from the great outdoors. Attach tiny pinecones—pristine or spruced up with metallic floral spray—to plain, solid-colored tags using glue. The pattern can be anything from a mini wreath to a pretty cluster. For the pine-needle tree, use a fine paintbrush to coat the needles with craft glue; then arrange them carefully with tweezers.

glittery greenery toppers

These natural sprigs and sprays get a stunning metallic finish. **1** Cover mistletoe berries with silver paint. **2** For a two-tone look, combine a natural magnolia leaf with one that's spray-painted silver. **3** Lightly dust a cedar sprig with spray adhesive, then dip in glitter. **4** Seeded eucalyptus turns sculptural when the leaves are painted with glue, then coated with glitter. **5** Make holly pop by silvering the berries. Paint berries with glue, then sprinkle with microbead glitter.

pipe cleaner gift toppers

A present is two treats in one when you decorate the package with soft handmade ornaments. Pipe cleaners (also known as chenille stems) are also easy for young children to work with; make a few extra decorations to keep for yourself.

WHAT YOU WILL NEED Pipe cleaners (in red, white, red terry, silver and red tinsel, 6mm green), hot-glue gun, glass beads or miniature ornaments, ribbon, pencil, cardboard, scissors, double-sided tape, red felt-tip marker, ruler, sequins

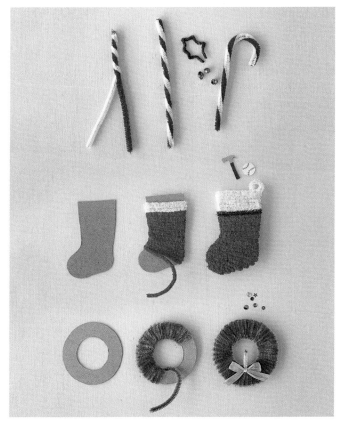

FOR THE CANDY CANES Twist together 5-inch-long red and white pipe cleaners. Make sure the stripes of the combined red-and-white pipe cleaners are neatly spaced. Curl the top into a hook. Bend a 3-inch length of a green pipe cleaner into the shape of a holly leaf; hot-glue the leaf in place, then hot-glue on a cluster of red beads for berries, or tie on a ribbon threaded with a tiny ornament.

FOR THE STOCKINGS Draw a stocking shape onto cardboard; cut out. Apply two strips of double-sided tape to the back (to hold the pipe cleaners in place). Beginning about ⅝ inch from the top, wrap the cardboard form with 6-inch red terry pipe cleaners, working from cuff line to toe; tuck in the ends on the back side. For the cuff, wrap the form with standard white pipe cleaners, working from the bottom up; curl up the end of the last piece to make a loop. Wrap a silver or red tinsel pipe cleaner around bottom of cuff, and hot-glue at each end. Glue beads or other miniature ornaments to the top edge. Or construct miniature stocking stuffers by hand from paper (or use stickers), mount to cardboard, and hot-glue to back of stocking so they seem to peek out of the top.

FOR THE WREATHS Cut a cardboard circle 3 inches in diameter. Cut a 1-inch-diameter circle out of its center. Wrap this wreath form tightly with the 6-millimeter green pipe cleaners; you'll need about four 12-inch pipe cleaners for each. To add a tiny candle, cut a 1-inch piece of white pipe cleaner; "light" the flame with a red felt-tip marker. With hot glue, attach to the wreath; glue a ribbon bow over it, and add sequins and beads to resemble ornaments.

pom-pom "flower" bows

Self-adhesive bows are standard fare in the world of gift wrap, but a few snips can turn them into something truly extraordinary. All you need to create lavish frills is a little imagination and a handful of basic crafting supplies.

WHAT YOU WILL NEED Sharp scissors, store-bought self-adhesive ribbon bows, ribbon, double-sided tape

Use sharp scissors to snip off the tip of each loop at an angle, rather than straight across the middle. Fill a large bow's bare middle with a smaller snipped bow (see above right), affixing it with its adhesive backing. Then fill its center with a matching ribbon loop attached with double-sided tape. Affix bow to box (atop ribbon binding, if desired) with its adhesive backing. If bow pops off, secure it with double-sided tape. .

yarn ties

Give holiday gifts a warming appeal by winding yarn around presents. Wrap a few times for thin stripes or several times more for thick ones. Combine different yarns for colorful striations. Knot strands tightly on the bottom of each box. If desired, tie a bow on top.

BASIC TECHNIQUES

crafts essentials

With the following in your crafts cupboard, you should be able to complete any project in this book.

TOOLS

- ASSORTED SCISSORS
  (*all-purpose scissors, fabric scissors, embroidery scissors, pinking shears*)
- SCREW PUNCH
- ADJUSTABLE CIRCLE CUTTER
- CRAFT KNIFE
- CUTTING MAT
- BONE FOLDER
- ASSORTED BRUSHES
  (*paintbrushes, foam craft brush, soft bristle brush*)
- WIRE CUTTERS
- NEEDLE-NOSE PLIERS
- RUBBER STAMPS
  AND STAMP MOUNTS
- RULER

SUPPLIES

- ASSORTED ADHESIVES
  (*white craft glue, tacky glue, clear fabric glue, hot-glue gun, double-sided tape*)
- TISSUE PAPER
- CARD STOCK
- GLITTER (*assorted colors*)
- PERMANENT MARKERS
- GEL-INK PENS
- COLORED PENCILS
- PAINT

using a screw punch

Traditional hole punches work only around the edges of a sheet of paper. To make a hole at any point on a sheet, use a screw punch (sometimes called a Japanese hole punch) instead. Cover your work surface with a cutting mat. Place paper on top. Insert the desired tip in the punch (most come with several sizes). Place the tip of the punch on the paper. Press down on the punch firmly until you can't push anymore, then release.

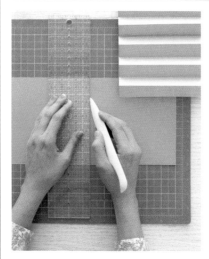

using a bone folder

To make perfect folds and creases for scrapbook pages, handcrafted cards, origami boxes, and more, first place a ruler on the paper where you want the fold. Hold the ruler firmly in place with one hand. Run the pointed tip of a bone folder along the length of the ruler, pressing it firmly down as you go. Remove the ruler and fold the paper along the scored line.

tying a bow on a package

1 Any present looks much prettier with a properly tied bow. Place the box facedown on the ribbon, positioning it so the ribbon runs the length of the box.

2 Draw the ribbon ends up, and tie—don't knot—pulling the ribbon taut.

3 Turn the box right-side up. Wrap the ribbon around the width of the box. Cross the ribbon.

4 Create two loops that are equal in size. Cross the right loop over the left.

5 Bring it under and through the hole. Pull the knot tight.

6 Adjust the loops and the tails, and trim the ends of the tails until they are the same length. Notch the ends, if desired, or trim them with pinking or scalloping shears (both will prevent fraying).

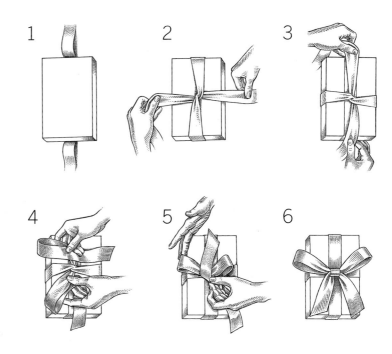

cutting with a craft knife

Cover your work surface with a cutting mat. Place paper or card stock on top, and place a ruler where you'd like to cut. Hold the ruler firmly in place with one hand. Run the pointed tip of a craft knife along the length of the ruler, dragging it very gently down as you go. This will lightly score the paper (you're not trying to cut through it yet), and leave a "path" for the blade to follow. While continuing to hold the ruler in place, draw the blade down the scored line, pressing a little harder to cut through the paper. Ignore your instincts: Pressing hard and dragging the knife will lead to crooked cuts and broken blades. If the paper starts to bunch and tear under the blade, it's time to replace your blade.

using a pom-pom maker

1 A pom-pom maker includes a set of horseshoe-shaped plastic templates with interlocking feet. (You could make one out of cardboard, but commercial versions, available at crafts stores in set sizes, are inexpensive and easier to work with.) Place two templates back to back, ends pointing outward.

2 Wind yarn around tool from end to end, more or less closely, depending on thickness desired for pom-pom. Repeat with remaining templates.

3 Snap the two templates together (figure 3 shows what the templates look like under the yarn).

4 Snip the yarn along the rounded ridge of each. Insert thread between open yarn ends around circumference of templates; tie firmly. Pull templates free. Fluff pompom into shape, and trim with scissors.

1 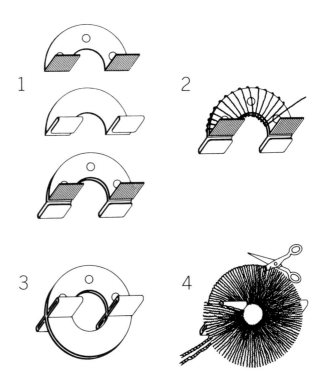 2

3  4

tying a classic bow

1

2

3

1 Create two loops, one on each side of the ribbon. Cross right loop over left.

2 Knot by passing right loop behind left, under, and up through (make sure ribbon is not twisted or bunched).

3 Pull loops to create a small, smooth knot. Adjust loops, opening them up with your fingers; cut notches in tails.

quilling basics

A simple twist is all it takes to make elegant loops, curls, coils, and hearts. Combine the different shapes to create elaborate designs. See pages 59 and 320 for specific quilling projects.

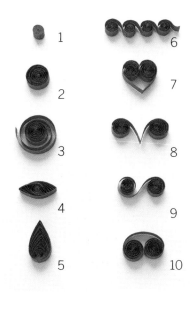

SHAPES GLOSSARY

By coiling paper around the quilling tool as shown below and following these instructions, you can make quilled designs in a variety of shapes and sizes.

1 TIGHT CIRCLE Slip paper into the slot on the quilling tool, and turn it until the paper forms a firm cylinder. Remove the paper from the tool, and glue it closed.

2 LOOSE CIRCLE Create a tight circle, but do not glue it. Instead, lay it on a flat surface, and let it expand. When you're satisfied with the shape and size, glue the end of the strip to secure it.

3 LOOSE SCROLL Form a loose circle, but do not glue it closed.

4 MARQUISE Fashion and glue a loose circle; pinch each end.

5 TEARDROP Create and glue a loose circle; pinch one end.

6 CONNECTED SCROLLS Make several loose scrolls. Position them with the unrolled ends pointing the same way. Curve each end over the rolled side of the next scroll; glue.

7 OPEN HEART Fold a strip in half, and crease it. Roll each end toward the center crease.

8 "V" SCROLL Crease the paper at the center; roll the ends outward.

9 "S" SCROLL Form an S shape by rolling one end toward the center, and the other in the opposite direction.

10 "C" SCROLL Roll both ends of a strip toward the center.

1 Hold the quilling paper in one hand and the quilling tool in the other. Slip the paper into the slot on the tool, placing the paper's end flush with the end of the slot.

2 Turn the tool until the strip is rolled into a firm cylinder. The desired shape (see glossary above) will determine how tight or loose to make the cylinder.

3 After you've achieved the desired shape, glue the end of the strip to secure it, if necessary. Use a round-headed pin to apply glue precisely. To make a marquise or a teardrop shape, as shown here, pinch and crease one or both ends after gluing.

embroidery basics

To begin, gather your tools: an embroidery needle, thread or yarn, the article to embroider (linen fabrics are best, but woven cotton, wool, and felt are suitable), a way to transfer the design (a heat-transfer pencil and tracing paper or an iron-on transfer design), and an embroidery hoop, to hold fabric taut. The standard thread is cotton floss, made of six separate strands (silk and rayon threads also come in divisible strands); use two for most woven fabrics. Yarn cannot be separated, though it comes in several weights; it's best for heavy fabrics.

BACKSTITCH This is the easiest stitch. Insert the needle from the wrong side of the fabric, coming out at 1. Insert needle at 2, pull back out at 3, and pull thread tight. Insert needle again at 1, and pull it out past 3 at a distance equal to the length of the previous stitches. This is the first step for the next stitch; insert needle into 3, and continue.

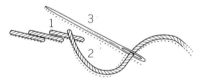

STEM STITCH A cousin to the backstitch, this stitch creates a ropelike effect. Insert needle from wrong to right side, coming out at 1. Insert the needle at 2 at a slight diagonal, and pull through at 3 (halfway between 1 and 2). Repeat stitching, keeping the thread on the left side of the needle and making sure all stitches are the same length.

CHAINSTITCH With your thread, insert the needle from the wrong to the right side, coming out at 1. Making a loop, insert next to 1. Come out again at 2, holding the thread under the needle as you pull tight. Insert the needle again next to 2 (inside the new link), and continue.

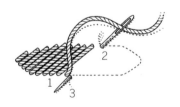

SATIN STITCH Made at an angle or straight across, these side-by-side stitches fill in the outlines of a design that incorporates shape or width. Insert the needle from the wrong to the right side, coming out at 1. Insert the needle at 2, and pull it back through at 3, right next to 1. Keep the stitches tight and flat to ensure a smooth finish.

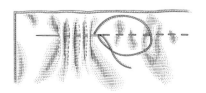

RUNNING STITCH Insert the needle several times at evenly spaced intervals, then pull the needle and thread through. Repeat.

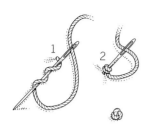

FRENCH KNOT Insert the needle from the wrong to the right side of the fabric at 1. Keeping the thread taut with one hand, use your other hand to wind it over the needle twice. Reinsert the tip of the needle into the fabric at 2, as close as possible to where it first emerged. Before passing the needle through the fabric, pull the thread tight so that the knot is flush with the material. Pull the needle through the fabric, continuing to hold the thread tight until you have a 3- to 4-inch (7.5–10 cm) loop, then let go, and finish the knot. For larger knots, wrap more than two times.

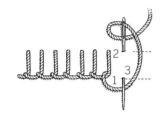

BLANKET STITCH If using as a decorative edge, work so that the base of the U goes along the edge of the fabric. For lightweight fabrics, stitch along the finished edge. Insert the needle from the wrong to the right side, coming out at 1. Insert at 2. Come out again at 3; hold the thread under the needle with your thumb as you pull tight.

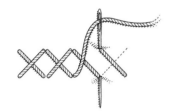

CROSS-STITCH First, stitch a row of evenly spaced parallel diagonal lines. Then stitch diagonally back over the first row, creating crosses as you go. When you can, insert the needle where Xs meet in the same holes. For the entire pattern, the bottom stitches on each X should all slant one way and the top stitches the other way.

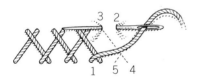

HERRINGBONE STITCH In this variation on the counted cross-stitch, threads overlap at the end rather than the center. Pull needle through to front at 1. Insert at 2, pulling it back out at 3, and pull thread tight. Cross over stitch and insert needle at 4 and pull back through at 5.

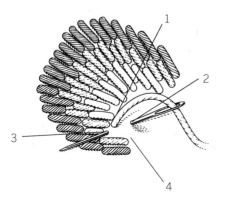

LONG AND SHORT STITCH Used to blend colors, or create a feathery texture. Insert needle from wrong to right side, coming out at 1; insert at 2, come out at 3; and insert again at 4. Repeat for next tier. If desired, change colors and use the same technique for the following tiers, piercing the stitches in the previous tier.

SOURCES

The following is a list of addresses that we hope will prove useful as you source the tools, materials and general craft supplies that you will need to complete the projects in this book. Many of the contacts provided are for suppliers of general equipment relating to the crafts featured in the book. However, wherever possible, we have provided contacts for specific project products. If you cannot find the exact product we have used, be flexible and adapt the project idea to suit the products available to you.

Note: All addresses, phone numbers and websites were verified at the time of publication, although, naturally, this information is subject to change.

basic crafts supplies

HOBBYCRAFT
Visit the website or phone for details of your nearest store.
tel: 01202 596100
www.hobbycraft.co.uk

HOMECRAFTS DIRECT
Hamilton House
Mountain Road
Leicester
LE4 9HQ
tel: 0116 2697733
email: info@homecrafts.co.uk
www.homecrafts.co.uk

PANDURO HOBBY
Westway House
Transport Avenue
Brentford
Middlesex
TW8 9HF
tel: 0845 121 6875
email: customer@panduro.co.uk
www.panduro.co.uk

RUCRAFT
tel: 0844 8805852
www.rucraft.co.uk

adhesives and glues

CRAFT CREATIONS
Ingersoll House
Delamore Road
Cheshunt
EN8 9HD
tel: 01992 781900
email: enquiries@craftcreations.com
www.craftcreations.com

HOBBYCRAFT
Visit the website or phone for details of your nearest store.
tel: 01202 596100
www.hobbycraft.co.uk

HOMECRAFTS DIRECT
Hamilton House
Mountain Road
Leicester
LE4 9HQ
tel: 0116 2697733
email: info@homecrafts.co.uk
www.homecrafts.co.uk

albums and scrapbooks

CALICO CRAFTS
tel: 01353 624100
www.calicocrafts.co.uk

THE CRAFTZ BOUTIQUE
Unit 15
Whitehill Ind Estate
Whitehill Lane
Wootton Bassett
Swindon
SN4 7DB
tel: 01793 859977 or 01793 790919
email: sales@thecraftzboutique.com
www.thecraftzboutique.com

beads and jewellery making supplies

BEADS DIRECT
tel: 01509 218028
email: service@beadsdirect.co.uk
www.beadsdirect.co.uk

THE BEAD SCENE STUDIO
Wakefield Country Courtyard
Wakefield Lodge Estate
Potterspury
NN12 7QX
tel: 01327 353639
email: stephanie@thebeadscene.com
www.thebeadscene.com

THE BUTTON LADY
16 Hollyfield Road South
Sutton Coldfield
West Midlands
B76 1NX
tel: 01213 293234
www.thebuttonlady.co.uk

DEBBIE CRIPPS
8 Christchurch Street West
Frome
Somerset
BA11 1EQ
tel: 01373 454448
www.debbiecripps.co.uk

GUTERMANN
Perivale-Gutermann Ltd.
Bullsbrook Road
Hayes
UB4 0JR
tel: 020 8589 1642
email: contact@guetermann.com
www.guetermann.com

JOSY ROSE LTD.
PO Box 44204
London
E3 3XB
tel: 0845 450 1212
email: info@josyrose.com
www.josyrose.com

KARS
tel: 0870 240 7993
email: salesuk@kars.eu
www.kars.biz

KERNOWCRAFT ROCKS & GEMS LTD.
Bolingey
Perranporth
TR6 0DH
tel: 01872 573888
email: info@kernowcraft.com
www.kernowcraft.com

RUCRAFT
tel: 0844 8805852
www.rucraft.co.uk

THE SPELLBOUND BEAD COMPANY
45 Tamworth Street
Lichfield
WS13 6JW
tel: 01543 417650
email: info@spellboundbead.co.uk
www.spellboundbead.co.uk

block printing supplies

LONDON GRAPHIC CENTRE
tel: 020 7759 4500
email: info@londongraphics.co.uk
www.londongraphics.co.uk

botanical pressing supplies

FRED ALDOUS LTD.
37 Lever Street
Manchester
M1 1LW
tel: 0161 236 4224
www.fredaldous.co.uk

calligraphy supplies

SCRIBBLERS
tel: 0845 003 7148
www.scribblers.co.uk

candlemaking supplies

CANDLEMAKERS SUPPLIES
Behind 102–104 Shepherds Bush Road
London
W6 7PD
tel: 07855 340132
email: mail@candlemakers.co.uk
www.candlemakers.co.uk

FULLMOONS CAULDRON
PO Box 2173
Ascot
SL5 0PQ
tel: 01344 627 945
www.fullmoons-cauldron.co.uk

china and glass paints

HOBBYCRAFT
Visit the website or phone for details of your nearest store.
tel: 01202 596100
www.hobbycraft.co.uk

LAINE'S FLORAL ART & HOBBY CRAFTS
60 Commerce Street
Insch
AB52 6JB
tel: 01464 820335
www.lainesworld.co.uk

PORCELAINE PAINTS
43 Old School Close
Codicote
Hitchin
SG4 8YJ
email: sales@porcelainpaint.co.uk
www.porcelainpaint.co.uk

clay (including polymer clay)

KARS
tel: 0870 240 7993
email: salesuk@kars.eu
www.kars.biz

clip art

THE CLIP ART WAREHOUSE
www.clipart.co.uk

cookie cutters and molds

For biscuit cutters and mini loaf pans
DE CUISINE
Spion House
Rushall Lane
Lytchett Matravers
Poole
BH16 6AJ
tel: 01202 620097
www.decuisine.co.uk

For molds and bakeware
LAKELAND
Visit the website or phone for details of your nearest store.
tel: 015394 88100
www.lakeland.co.uk

cutting tools

CRAFT CREATIONS
Ingersoll House
Delamore Road
Cheshunt
EN8 9HD
tel: 01992 781900
email: enquiries@craftcreations.com
www.craftcreations.com

dyeing and printing supplies

FRED ALDOUS LTD.
37 Lever Street
Manchester
M1 1LW
tel: 0161 236 4224
www.fredaldous.co.uk

KBT LTD.
Carlton Business Centre
132 Saltley Road
Saltley
Birmingham
B7 4TH
tel: 0870 350 1936
www.dyeshop.co.uk

fabric paints

DYLON
Spotless Punch Ltd.
Knowles House
Cromwell Road
Redhill
RH1 1RT
tel: 01737 742020
email: info@dylon.co.uk
www.dylon.co.uk

FIBRECRAFTS
Old Portsmouth Road
Peasmarsh
Guildford
Surrey
GU3 1LZ
www.fibrecrafts.com

fabric supplies

BACKSTITCH
10 Tucker Street
Wells
Somerset
BA5 2DZ
tel: 01749 675 272
email: enq@backstitch.co.uk
www.backstitch.co.uk

CALICO LAINE
Visit the website for details of your nearest store.
tel: 01513 363939
www.calicolaine.co.uk

CHEAPFABRICS
Thames Court
1 Victoria Street
Windsor
Berkshire
SL4 1YB
www.cheapfabrics.co.uk

FABRIC LAND
Fabric Towers
Kingfisher Park
Headland
Salisbury Road
Ringwood
BH24 3NX
www.fabricland.co.uk

JOHN LEWIS
*Visit the website or phone for
details of your nearest store.*
tel: 0845 604 9049
www.johnlewis.com

LIBERTY
Regent Street
London
W1B 5AH
tel: 02075 73 9645
www.liberty.co.uk

THE COTTON PATCH
1285 Stratford Road
Hall Green
Birmingham
B28 9AJ
tel: 0121 702 2840
email: mailorder@cottonpatch.net
www.cottonpatch.co.uk

For sepia and country fabrics
ANTIQUE ANGEL
21 Thomas More buildings
10 Ickenham Road
Ruislip
HA4 7BA
tel: 07765 888136
email: kylie@antiqueangel.co.uk
www.antiqueangel.co.uk

*For plain and patterned cotton
fabrics and haberdashery
trimmings*
CHAWLA'S
tel: 0208 572 2902
www.efabrics.co.uk

For vintage and new fabrics
DONNA FLOWER
www.donnaflower.com

For Japanese fabrics and threads
EURO JAPAN LINKS LTD.
32 Nant Road
Childs Hill
London
NW1 2AT
tel: 0208 201 9324
www.eurojapanlinks.co.uk

*For end of line retail fabrics,
including designer names*
FABRICS GALORE
52-54 Lavender Hill
Battersea
London
SW11 5RH
www.fabricsgalore.co.uk

For funky and retro fabrics
GAGA FABRICS
108 Main Road
Gedling
Nottingham
NG4 3HE
tel: 0115 841 8898
www.gagafabrics.co.uk

For organic, fair-trade fabrics
GREEN FIBRES
99 High Street
Totnes
Devon
TQ9 5PF
www.greenfibres.co.uk

For Batik fabrics
HANNAH'S ROOM
50 Church Street
Brierley
Barnsley
South Yorkshire
S72 9HT
tel: 01226 713427
email: sales@hannahsroom.co.uk
www.hannahsroom.co.uk

For linen fabrics
LINEN ME LTD.
23 Glendale Close
St Johns
Woking
GU21 3HN
tel: 0208 133 3853
www.linenme.com

*For organic and sustainable fabrics,
including cotton and hemp*
LOOP FABRICS
32 West Hill Road
Brighton
BN1 3RT
www.loopfabric.co.uk

For bridal and occasion fabrics
MILLCROFT TEXTILES
tel: 01159 263154
www.millcrofttextiles.co.uk

*For beautiful and unusual Japanese
cotton fabrics*
MISFORMAKE
www.misformake.co.uk

*For vintage Japanese textiles, kits
and patterns*
SUSAN BRISCOE DESIGNS
Yamadera
4 Mount Zion
Brymbo
Wrexham
LL11 5NB
www.susanbriscoe.co.uk

For African fabrics and trims
THE AFRICAN FABRIC SHOP
19 Hebble Mount
Meltham
Holmfirth
West Yorkshire
HD9 4HG
tel: 01484 850188
email: magie@africanfabric.co.uk
www.africanfabric.co.uk

frames and framing materials

For framing materials
HOBBYCRAFT
Visit the website or phone for details of your nearest store.
tel: 01202 596100
www.hobbycraft.co.uk

For frames
IKEA
Visit the website for details of your local store.
www.ikea.com

furniture and accessories

For wooden furniture, desk tidies and wooden hangers ideal for decorating
IKEA
Visit the website for details of your local store.
www.ikea.com

For a range of high-quality furniture and accessory blanks
SCUMBLE GOOSIE
Griffin Mill
London Road
Thrupp
Gloucestershire
GL5 2AZ
tel: 01453 731305
email: enquiries@scumblegoosie.com
www.scumblegoosie.com

gilding supplies

ALEC TIRANTI LTD.
3 Pipers Court
Berkshire Drive
Thatcham
RG19 4ER
tel: 0845 123 2100
email: enquiries@tiranti.co.uk
www.tiranti.co.uk

glass etching

HOBBY'S
W Hobby Ltd.
Knight's Hill Square
London
SE27 0HH
tel: 020 8761 4244
www.hobby.uk.com

glitter

THE CRAFT BARN
9 East Grinstead Road
Lingfield
RH7 6EP
tel: 01342 836398
email: info@thecraftbarn.com
www.thecraftbarn.com

CRAFTS U LOVE
Unit 1, Westcoats Farm
Stan Hill
Charlwood
Horley
RH6 0ES
tel: 01293 863 576
email: enquiries@craftsulove.co.uk
www.craftsulove.co.uk

jewellery making supplies

THE BEAD SHOP
21a Tower Street
Covent Garden
London
WC2H 9NS
tel: 020 7240 0931
email: customerservice@beadworks.co.uk
www.beadworks.co.uk

CREATIVE BEADCRAFT LTD.
Unit 2
Asheridge Business Centre
Asheridge Road
Chesham
HP5 2PT
tel: 01494 778 818
email: tracey@creativebeadcraft.co.uk
www.creativebeadcraft.co.uk

RUCRAFT
tel: 0844 8805852
www.rucraft.co.uk

journals and notebooks

PAPERCHASE
Visit the website for details of your nearest store.
www.paperchase.co.uk

light sensitive printing

For light sensitive (blue print) fabric
RAINBOW SILKS
6 Wheelers Yard
High Street
Great Missenden
HP16 0AL
tel: 01494 862111
email: caroline@rainbowsilks.co.uk
www.rainbowsilks.co.uk

For light sensitive (sunprint) paper
HAWKIN'S BAZAAR
Visit the website or phone for details of your nearest store.
tel: 0844 557 5261
www.hawkin.com

marbleizing

FRED ALDOUS LTD.
37 Lever Street
Manchester
M1 1LW
tel: 0161 236 4224
www.fredaldous.co.uk

memory foil tape

CHEDDAR STAMPER
14 Mansfield Lane
Calverton
Nottingham
NG14 6HL
tel: 0115 938 4711
www.cheddarstamper.co.uk

mosaics supplies

MOSAIC TRADER UK
Unit 15a
Barton Business Park
New Dover Road
Canterbury
CT1 3AA
tel: 01227 781601
email: info@mosaictraderuk.com
www.mosaictraderuk.com

nature crafts

For dried and decorative materials for floral arrangements including wreaths and pine cones
THE ESSENTIALS COMPANY
tel: 01379 608899
email: info@essentialscompany.co.uk
www.theessentialscompany.co.uk

For pressed flowers and leaves
CROFT PETALS
The Old Dairy Barn
Dunmow Road
Beauchamp Roding
Nr Ongar
CM5 0PF
tel: 01279 876542
email: sales@croftmetalwork.co.uk
www.croftpetals.co.uk

For shells
EATON'S SEASHELLS
tel: 01279 410284
www.eatonsseashells.co.uk

paper

For a wide range of decorative papers
MY PAPER WAREHOUSE
Grosvenor House Papers Ltd.
Westmorland Business Park
Kendal
LA9 6NP
tel: 01539 726161
email: info@ghpkendal.co.uk
www.mypaperwarehouse.co.uk

PAPERCHASE
Visit the website for details of your nearest store.
www.paperchase.co.uk

RUCRAFT
tel: 0844 8805852
www.rucraft.co.uk

For card blanks and stationery
THE CRAFT BARN
9 East Grinstead Road
Lingfield
RH7 6EP
tel: 01342 836398
email: info@thecraftbarn.com
www.thecraftbarn.com

For Japanese and origami papers
JAPAN CENTRE
14–16 Regent Street
London
SW1Y 4PH
tel: 020 3405 1150
email: bookshop_manager
@japancentre.com
www.japancentre.com

For wood veneer paper
CRAFTY COMPUTER PAPER
Hamilton House
Mountain Road
Leicester
LE4 9HQ
tel: 0844 809 9535
email: sales@craftycomputerpaper.
co.uk
www. craftycomputerpaper.co.uk

paper punches

THE ART OF CRAFT
101 Lynchford Road
North Camp
Farnborough
GU14 6ET
tel: 01252 377677
email: info@art-of-craft.co.uk
www.art-of-craft.co.uk

RUCRAFT
tel: 0844 8805852
www.rucraft.co.uk

photo craft supplies

For magnetic paper
POLARITY MAGNETS
Unit 3b
Sopwith Crescent
Wickford Business Park
Wickford
SS11 8YU
tel: 01268 768 768
www.magnetick.co.uk

For photo paper
FOTOSPEED DISTRIBUTION
Unit 6B
Park Lane Industrial Estate
Corsham
SN13 9LG
tel: 01249 714555
email: info@fotospeed.com
www.fotospeed.com

For printer-ready fabric sheets
CRAFTY COMPUTER PAPER
Hamilton House
Mountain Road
Leicester
LE4 9HQ
tel: 0844 809 9535
email: sales@craftycomputerpaper.
co.uk
www. craftycomputerpaper.co.uk

plate hangers

WARES OF KNUTSFORD LTD.
PO Box 321
Knutsford
WA16 8YQ
tel: 08456 121273
email: sales@waresofknutsford.co.uk
www.waresofknutsford.co.uk

polymer clay

see clay

polystyrene shapes

LAINE'S FLORAL ART & HOBBY CRAFTS
60 Commerce Street
Insch
AB52 6JB
tel: 01464 820335
www.lainesworld.co.uk

pom-pom maker

SEW AND SO
Unit 8A
Chalford Industrial Estate
Stroud
GL6 8NT
tel: 01453 889988
email: sales@sewandso.co.uk
www.sewandso.co.uk

quilling

FRED ALDOUS LTD.
37 Lever Street
Manchester
M1 1LW
tel: 0161 236 4224
www.fredaldous.co.uk

J.J. QUILLING DESIGN
29 Hollingworth Road
Petts Wood
Orpington
Kent
BR5 1AQ
tel: 020 8295 1822
www.jjquilling.co.uk

ribbon and cord

THE COTTON PATCH
1285 Stratford Road
Hall Green
Birmingham
B28 9AJ
tel: 0121 702 2840
email: mailorder@cottonpatch.net
www.cottonpatch.co.uk

CRAFTS U LOVE
Unit 1, Westcoats Farm
Stan Hill
Charlwood
Horley
RH6 OES
tel: 01293 863 576
email: enquiries@craftsulove.co.uk
www.craftsulove.co.uk

CRAFTY RIBBONS
3 Beechwood Clump Farm
Tin Pot Lane
Blandford
DT11 7TD
tel: 01258 455889
email: info@craftyribbons.com
www.craftyribbons.com

rope

ROPE LOCKER
Mylor Yacht Harbour
Falmouth
TR11 5UF
tel: 0117 230 8525
www.ropelocker.co.uk

rub-on letters and borders

LETRASET LTD.
Kingsnorth Industrial Estate
Wotton Road
Ashford
TN23 6FL
tel: 01233 624421
email: enquiries@letraset.com
www.letraset.com

rubber stamping supplies

THE CRAFT BARN
9 East Grinstead Road
Lingfield
RH7 6EP
tel: 01342 836398
email: info@thecraftbarn.com
www.thecraftbarn.com

PERSONAL IMPRESSIONS
Curzon Road
Chilton Industrial Estate
Sudbury
CO10 2XW
*Visit the website for details
of local stockists.*
tel: 01787 375241
email: customerservices@
personalimpressions.com
www.personalimpressions.com

RUCRAFT
tel: 0844 8805852
www.rucraft.co.uk

WHICHCRAFT
The Corn Exchange
Craft Gallery
Doncaster
DN1 1QZ
tel: 01302 369666
email: info@whichcraftuk.co.uk
www.whichcraft.co.uk

sewing machines

JANOME
*Visit the website for details
of your nearest stockist.*
tel: 01616 666011
www.janome.co.uk

BROTHER INTERNATIONAL
*Visit the website for details of your
nearest stockist.*
tel: 0844 499 9444
www.brothersewing.eu

*For machines and attachments
for all major brands*
SEWING MACHINES DIRECT
*Visit the website for details of
your nearest store.*
tel: 0800 092 5215
www.sewingmachines.co.uk

THE SEWING MACHINE SHOP
1 The Broadway
Brighton Road
Worthing
West Sussex
BN11 3EG
tel: 01903 200771
email: sales@sewingmachineshop.co.uk
www.sewingmachineshop.co.uk

sewing supplies

COAST AND COUNTRY CRAFTS
Cornish Garden Nurseries
Barras Moor Farm
Perranarworthal
Truro
Cornwall
TR3 7PE
www.coastandcountrycrafts.co.uk

DMC CREATIVE WORLD LTD.
1st Floor Compass Building
Feldspar Close
Enderby
Leicestershire
LE19 4SD
tel: 01162 754000
www.dmccreative.co.uk

JAYCOTTS
Unit D2
Chester Trade Park
Bumpers Lane
Chester
CH1 4LT
tel: 01244 394099
www.jaycotts.co.uk

LEXI LOVES
57 Cricklade St
Crencester
Gloucestershire
GL7 1HY
tel: 01285 655452
email: lexiloves@o2email.co.uk
www.lexilovesshop.com

SEW AND SO
Stroud House
Russell Street
Stroud
Gloucestershire
GL5 3AN
tel: 01453 889988
email: salesteam@sewandso.co.uk
www.sewandso.co.uk

SEW BOX
63 Parkside
London
SE3 7QF
email: contact@sewbox.co.uk
www.sewbox.co.uk

SEW ESSENTIAL LTD.
Burleigh House
2 Box Street
Walsall
West Midlands
WS1 2JR
tel: 01922 722276
email: enquiries@sewessential.co.uk
www.sewessential.co.uk

SEWING ONLINE
9 Mallard Rd
Victoria Business Park
Netherfield
Nottingham
NG4 2PE
tel: 01159 874422
email: sales@sewing-online.co.uk
www.sewing-online.com

THE MAKE LOUNGE
49-51 Barnsbury Street
London
N1 1TP
tel: 0207 609 0275
email: create@themakelounge.com
www.themakelounge.com

THE SEWING STUDIO
5 Green Lane
Redruth
TR15 1JY
tel: 01209 216942
www.thesewingstudio.co.uk

For fabrics, haberdashery and patchworking materials
DOUGHTY'S
tel: 01432 352546
www.doughtysonline.co.uk

For millinery wire, fabrics and haberdashery
MACCULLOCH AND WALLIS
25-26 Dering Street
London
W1S 1AT
tel: 02076 290311
www.macculloch-wallis.co.uk

For wool felt, haberdashery and craft fabric
THE ETERNAL MAKER
89 Oving Road
Chichester
West Sussex
PO19 7EW
www.eternalmaker.co.uk

For fabrics, threads, patterns and general sewing supplies
TRURO FABRICS
tel: 01872 222 130
www.trurofabrics.com

silkscreening supplies

LONDON GRAPHIC CENTRE
tel: 020 7759 4500
email: info@londongraphics.co.uk
www.londongraphics.co.uk

soap making supplies

SOAP BASICS
Mail order only:
23 Southbrook Road
Melksham
SN12 8DS
tel: 01225 899286
email: info@soapbasics.co.uk
www.soapbasics.co.uk

tin punching

For 28-gauge (0.3mm) metal sheets
THE CRAZY WIRE COMPANY
tel: 01925 406602
www.crazywireco.co.uk

vinyl, clear iron-on

Distributors of HeatnBond iron-on vinyl

BRAMWELL CRAFTS
Innovation Centre
1 Evolution Park
Haslingden Road
Blackburn
BB1 2FD
Visit the website for details of local stockists.
tel: 0844 243 4800
email: info@bramwellcrafts.co.uk
www.bramwellcrafts.co.uk

wirework

WIRES.CO.UK
Unit 3, Zone A
Chelmsford Road Industrial Estate
Great Dunmow
Essex
CM6 1HD
tel: 01371 238013
www.wires.co.uk

yarns

ARTESANO
5-9 Berkeley Avenue
Reading
RG1 6EL
tel: 01189 503350
www.artisanoyarns.co.uk

COLINETTE YARNS
Units 2–5
Banwy Industrial Estate
Llanfair Caereinion
Powys
SY21 0SG
tel: 01938 552141
www.colinette.com

CUCUMBER PATCH LTD.
59 High Street
Wolstanton
Newcastle under Lyme
Staffordshire
ST5 0ER
tel: 01782 862332
email: sales@cucumberpatch.co.uk
www.cucumberpatch.co.uk

DESIGNER YARNS LTD.
Units 8–10 Newbridge Industrial Estate
Pitt Street
Keighley
BD21 4PQ
tel: 01535 664222
www.designeryarns.uk.com

JAEGAR HANDKNITS
Green Lane Mill
Holmfirth
West Yorks
HD9 2DX
tel: 01484 680050

ROWAN
Green Lane Mill
Holmfirth
West Yorks
HD9 2DX
tel: 01484 681881
email: info@knitrowan.com
www.knitrowan.com

SIRDAR SPINNING LTD.
Flanshaw Lane
Alvethorpe
Wakefield
WF2 9ND
tel: 01924 371501
www.sirdar.co.uk

TWILLEYS OF STAMFORD
Roman Mill
Little Casterton Road
Stamford
Lincolnshire
PE9 1BG
tel: 01780 752661
www.twilleys.co.uk

VIRTUAL YARNS
42 Gress
Isle of Lewis
HS2 0NB
www.virtualyarns.com

CLIP ART AND TEMPLATES

On the following pages, you'll find thumbnail images of all the clip art and templates included in the book, in the order in which they appear. To download the templates and clip art, go to our website, marthastewart.com/holiday-crafts-book-extras. Unless otherwise indicated in project instructions, templates can be printed on standard copy paper. Clip-art is often best printed on heavyweight photo print paper, such as that made by Epson.

PAPER-CONE PARTY FAVORS
New Year's (p. 18)

BEJEWELED HEART-SHAPED BOX
Valentine's Day (p. 37)

LOVE-KNOT BRACELETS
Valentine's Day (p. 38)

EMBROIDERED VALENTINES
Valentine's Day (p. 50)

EMBROIDERED VALENTINES
Valentine's Day (p. 50)

FOLDING HEART VALENTINE
Valentine's Day (p. 54)

BIG-EARED BUNNY
Easter (p. 69)

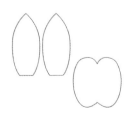

POM-POM BUNNIES AND THREAD-WRAPPED CARROTS
Easter (p. 72)

BUNNY GARLAND, CUPCAKE FLAGS, AND FAVOR BAGS
Easter (p. 74)

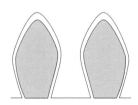

ENVELOPE BUNNY TREAT BAGS
Easter (p. 77)

SILHOUETTE DECOUPAGE EGGS
Easter (p. 88)

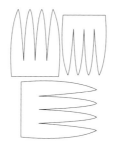

FLOWERY NOTES
Easter (p. 106)

CREPE PAPER CARROTS
Easter (p. 110)

HAND-EMBROIDERED BOTANICAL CARDS
Mother's Day (p. 117)

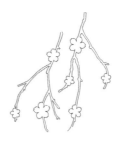

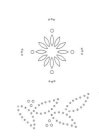

POP-UP BOUQUET CARD
Mother's Day (p. 120)

ENVELOPE SACHETS
Mother's Day (p. 126)

IRON-ON TRANSFER TOTE
Mother's Day (p. 134)

BATIK-STYLE TABLE LINENS
Mother's Day (p. 136)

CUSTOM CANVAS BAG
Mother's Day (p. 137)

CLIP ART FOOD LABELS
Father's Day (p. 141)

EMBELLISHED GAME BOX
Father's Day (p. 142)

NECKTIE ENVELOPE
Father's Day (p. 146)

CUSTOMIZED COUPONS
Father's Day (p. 150)

JACKET LAPEL CARD
Father's Day (p. 152)

PHOTO FRAME CARD
Father's Day (p. 153)

TISSUE-PAPER PENDANTS
Fourth of July (p. 170)

INDEPENDENCE DAY INVITES AND FAVORS
Fourth of July (p. 172)

CARVED BLACK PUMPKIN
Halloween (p. 181)

CARVED-PUMPKIN SILHOUETTES
Halloween (p. 186)

CARVED-PUMPKIN VILLAGE
Halloween (p. 188)

SILLY PUMPKIN FACES
Halloween (p. 194)

PATCH-O'-LANTERNS
Halloween (p. 198)

DASTARDLY TABLE DECORATIONS AND PAPER SPIDERWEBS
Halloween (p. 202)

BIRD SILHOUETTE WINDOW DECORATIONS
Halloween (p. 204)

JAR-O'-LANTERNS
Halloween (p. 208)

VAMPIRE BAT PIÑATA
Halloween (p. 210)

BATTY BAG CLIPS
Halloween (p. 215)

ILLUMINATED TRICK-OR-TREAT BAG
Halloween (p. 216)

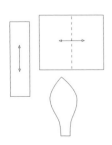

CORNHUSK-FLOWER NAPKIN RING
Thanksgiving (p. 223)

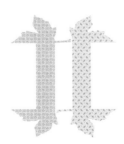

CLIP-ART LEAVES
Thanksgiving (p. 230)

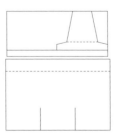

PAPER PILGRIM HAT AND BONNET
Thanksgiving (p. 246)

POM-POM TOMS
Thanksgiving (p. 250)

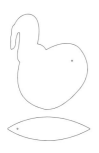

TURKEY TRIVIA
Thanksgiving (p. 253)

WRAPPED GELT
Hanukkah (p. 257)

DREIDEL GIFT CARD HOLDER
Hanukkah (p. 265)

POP-UP SYMBOLS
Hanukkah (p. 264)

GELT FAVOR BOXES
Hanukkah (p. 265)

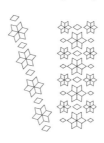

**STAR-PUNCHED
HURRICANE VASES**
Hanukkah (p. 266)

**MANZANITA-BRANCH
MENORAH**
Hanukkah (p. 268)

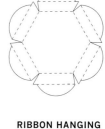

**RIBBON HANGING
CANDY-BASKET ORNAMENTS**
Christmas (p. 277)

**BEADED CINNAMON
BIRD ORNAMENTS**
Christmas (p. 286)

**GLITTERED
PAPER ORNAMENTS**
Christmas (p. 290)

CALLING-BIRD STOCKINGS
Christmas (p. 296)

**CANDY BASKET
CENTERPIECE**
Christmas (p. 306)

POP-UP CARDS
Christmas (p. 322)

CANDY CANE MICE
Christmas (p. 328)

**MONEY AND
GIFT CARD WRAPPERS**
Christmas (p. 330)

**HOLLY BLOCK-
PRINTED LINENS**
Christmas (p. 332)

INDEX

Page numbers in italics indicate illustrations.

ACKNOWLEDGMENTS

Many people contributed to the creation of this wonderful book, particularly our crafts editors, led by Editorial Director Marcie McGoldrick. The very talented crafters who contributed projects and ideas include Hannah Milman, Megen Lee, Jodi Levine, Silke Stoddard, Shane Powers, Athena Preston, Blake Ramsey, Stephanie Hung, Corrine Gill, Nicholas Andersen, and Laura Normandin. Thanks as well to Laura Kaesshafer for her support.

The special projects group at MSLO worked diligently to put all of the material into a comprehensive volume. They include Editorial Director Ellen Morrissey, Design Director William van Roden, editors Lindsey Stanberry and Stephanie Fletcher, and art directors Jeffrey Kurtz and Jessi Blackham. Catherine Gilbert compiled the voluminous images, Laura Wallis lent her editing talents, and Megan Rice provided invaluable editorial support. Creative Director Eric A. Pike gave invaluable guidance to the special projects team, as always.

We are grateful to many others at Martha Stewart Living Omnimedia, particularly Denise Clappi, Alison Vanek Devine, Heloise Goodman, Erin Fagerland, Johnny Miller, Ayesha Patel, Sarah Smart, and Gael Towey. And many heartfelt thanks to our publishing partners at Potter Craft— Victoria Craven, Joy Aquilino, Caitlin Harpin, Jess Morphew, Marysarah Quinn, Patricia Shaw, Amy Boorstein, Alyn Evans, Derek Gullino, Lauren Shakely, and Maya Mavjee—for their enthusiasm for the content and their overall support.

PHOTO CREDITS

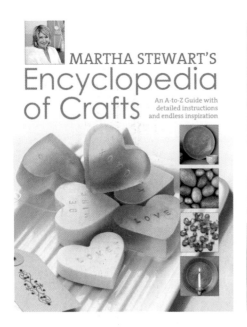